MENTAL MODELS

33 thinking tools to improve decision making, logical-analysis, problem-solving and discover the mindfulness secrets of the general thinking models increasing your brain power.

BY G.S. Baker

Table of Contents

Download the Audio Book Version of This Book for FREE

If you love listening to audio books on-the-go, I have great news for you. You can download the audio book version of this book for FREE just by signing up for a FREE 30-day audible trial! See below for more details!

Audible Trial Benefits

As an audible customer, you will receive the below benefits with your 30-day free trial:

- FREE audible book copy of this book
- After the trial, you will get 1 credit each month to use on any audiobook
- Your credits automatically roll over to the next month if you don't use them
- Choose from Audible's 200,000 + titles
- Listen anywhere with the Audible app across multiple devices
- Make easy, no-hassle exchanges of any audiobook you don't love
- Keep your audiobooks forever, even if you cancel your membership
- And much more

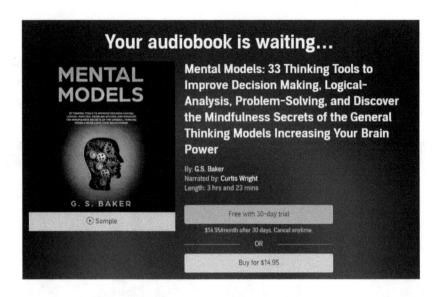

Click the links below to get started!

For Audible US

For Audible UK

For Audible FR

For Audible DE

INTRODUCTION

You may have heard the phrase, "What you see is the thing that you get." It suggests that our perspective on the world inhibits our ability to experience it. Maybe a couple would contend with the way that an individual who has never experienced love in their lives has a great deal of trouble finding, keeping up, or continuing a top of the line relationship. Along these lines if you've experienced childhood in contemptible neediness, it takes a great deal of personal change before you can live with wealth effectively. This book investigates the similarities between the spiritualist tradition of "the power of the mind " and the logical or hierarchical development tradition of "mental models." We all need something. Toying with these ideas drives us not far off where we are bound to get it.

Changing the awful to the high utilizing the power of our minds has been a point that surfaces intermittently through humanity's history. The latest and far-reaching structure has been the motion picture The Secret and the proliferation of some generally excellent educators, for example, Jerry and Esther Hicks. People who work with the power of the mind expand upon the idea that the 'intuitive' may likewise enable us to be in contact with the life force of the universe. Through reflection, and different procedures that open our awareness to more than what we know about in our constrained structure, we will approach ideas that take our lives in new and unforeseen bearings. Jerry and Esther Hicks add the feeling to this blend and instruct us that our 'enthusiastic direction framework' dependably fills us in as to whether we are on track with ourselves by whether we experience happiness and softness in our lives.

Mental models can be followed back to the work of Kenneth Craik in 1943 when he suggested that the human mind builds little scale models of reality that it uses to envision occasions. He proceeded to suggest that mental model can be developed from observation, our creative mind, or the standards of the lives we lead in the times we live. The intriguing point here is that mental models tie near visual images and can be unique. Have you at any point taken a gander at an illustration of somebody's idea, and "get it "instantly? That is the power of the mental model. Jay Wright Forrester characterized them as:

"The image of the world around us, which we convey in our mind, is only a model. No one in his mind envisions all the world, government, or nation. He has just chosen ideas, and connections among them, and utilizations those to speak to the genuine framework."

While Senge clarifies:

"Mental models are profoundly imbued suppositions, speculations, or even pictures or images that impact how we comprehend the world and how we make a move."

What is regular to both of these is the idea that until we understand the breaking points of our reasoning or mental models, we can't change them. When aware, our ability to make a move on new ideas is significantly upgraded.

Assembling everything

What is the helpfulness of these ideas? Regardless of whether we phrase it the power of mind or a mental model, our initial step is to perceive the imperatives we have in our lives because of how we think. Similarly, as we couldn't have envisioned the lives that we so effectively live today associated with people over the world a minor 30 years prior, we have to open to the idea that the potential that life could be substantially more tremendous and significantly more fascinating than we can envision today. Jerry and Esther Hicks would remind us that if we are involved in things that don't feel great, we are out of association with our most noteworthy potential. The people who work with corporate mental models likewise suggest that if we can't move beyond how we think now, we will ever have the option to open up to the new potentials around us.

My inquiry is, what might occur if vast gatherings of people started to structure the lives they needed for this planet genuinely? Imagine a scenario where, as opposed to concentrating on the weakening of nature, we focused on structure Paradise on Earth. Consider the possibility that as opposed to spending billions on our comprehension of sick wellbeing, we create examine those things that make wellbeing. Imagine a scenario in which those of us who are not kidding about structure associated network turned into the standard instead of the particular case. What sort of world do you imagine for your kids and grandkids? How might we center our mental models, or the power of our minds, to make only that?

CHAPTER ONE

What Clear Thinking is All About?

There is, by all accounts, a ton of disarray and free pondering stress in well-known diaries and books. By what another method would you be able to clarify terms like "good stress" and ideas like "A specific amount of stress is good for you," or counsel like "Stress is unavoidable." Once you comprehend the significance of stress, you'll understand that stress is continuously harmful, that there is no "sheltered" level of stress, and that you can divert pressure if you know how. How about we start by fixing the meaning of stress: pressure is certifiably not a psychological or passionate state, and it's positively not a right or otherworldly issue. Stress is a physiological and ailment, delivered by prolonged feelings of instability and anxiety.

Physical and Mental Symptoms

The Japanese word, "karoshi" means, roughly, "passing by stress," and it's a significant wellspring of mortality among Japanese workers, particularly moderately aged desk men. Stress kills them either straightforwardly, by making their bodies separate, or in a roundabout way, through melancholy and suicide. In either case, stress is awful news, and it's no distortion to state that your life is in question in a stressful situation. Perpetual stress influences your heart and conduits, your stomach related system, your skin and hair, your safe system, and your brain and sensory system, and every other organ in your body.

Stress is additionally ensnared in an assortment of psychological wellness disorders, including melancholy, anxiety, burnout, substance misuse, workplace and aggressive behavior at home, and suicide. Also, although stress hasn't been shown to cause personality disorders like schizophrenia, it complicates them and makes them increasingly difficult to treat.

Constant stress is a noteworthy health issue and is nothing to trifle with. To put it gruffly, stress can kill you as without a doubt as malignant growth.

Our Biological Inheritance

If stress is so harmful, why on the planet would we say we are so defenseless to it? Wouldn't you believe that advancement would have dispensed with it? It could be said, stress was designed a great many years prior, long before we ended up human, as an adjustment to living in a dangerous world. To clarify this oddity, how about we envision one of our long-back progenitors on the fields of Africa who all of a sudden turn upward and sees a leopard on the branch over his head. In considerably less than a large portion of a moment, with no conscious idea, his brain enrolls the image of the leopard and classifies it as a life-undermining danger.

At that point, the brain starts to mobilize the body either to run away or for the guard.

Fight or Flight?

At the point when the brain sees the leopard in the tree and decides that it is dangerous, it sends a sign to the adrenal organs, which sit over your kidneys. In response, the adrenal organs produce two hormones: first adrenaline and later cortisol. Adrenaline acts all around quickly on pretty much all aspects of your body. Your heart starts to pulsate all the more quickly and unequivocally, the little veins in your skin contract (that is the reason you look "white as a sheet" after you're terrified), your stomach quits processing nourishment, and your vision straight to a "burrow." These changes make you, for a brief period, more grounded and faster than you ordinarily are - prepared to run far from the leopard.

As you're running far from the leopard, the adrenal organs start to create a hormone called cortisol. Cortisol acts to build the amount of sugar in your blood for brisk energy, and if you need to flee for quite a long time and days without nourishment, cortisol enables your body to change over muscle and bone into energy. The consolidated impact of adrenaline and cortisol is to give us the strength we have to manage dangerous situations - and that is the reason we advanced the fight/flight response in any case.

Where Does Stress Come In?

For whatever length of time that your body is reacting to a leopard in a tree, everything is fine: you run away, and the stress hormones start to vanish following an hour or somewhere in the vicinity. Be that as it may, if you can neither run far from the danger nor fight it, at that point, the levels of stress hormones never go down. The adrenaline continues making your heart beat hard, and the cortisol holds separating muscle and bone to keep your glucose high. If this continues for a considerable length of time at once, you will start to feel the impacts: changes in your rest and eating designs, exclusive focus, unusual tiredness, and general anxiety and uneasiness. What we generally call stress is your impression of your body's physical reactions to raised hormones.

For what reason Does Work Cause Stress?

"Well," you may ask, "That is all decent about reacting to the leopard in the tree, yet for what reason does my work trigger a stress reaction - I haven't seen any leopards about." It appears that the brain isn't very complex about perceiving danger: it responds to a furious supervisor, or a forthcoming deadline, or an office menace in merely how it would return to the leopard: it starts to mobilize the stress hormones to either fight or run away. Be that as it may, in the workplace you can't do possibly one - you can't punch individuals in the nose, and you need to return tomorrow, regardless of whether you would prefer not to. This blend of seeing danger and not having the option to take care of business triggers job stress, and it won't stop until you can either fight or flee.

More Control Means Less Stress

If the absence of control makes stress more terrible, at that point, it pursues that being in control counters stress. "Being in control" means different things to different individuals. For certain workers, it just means getting the chance to decide when they take their breaks and to have some adaptability in planning. For other people, it means getting the opportunity to choose how to take care of business: what request to machine the parts or how to process the structures generally effectively. Be that as it may, for all workers, getting the chance to make choices about how and when to carry out their responsibility reduces the feeling of danger, brings down stress, and improves health.

Learning Conquers Stress

Many, numerous studies show that a standout amongst the best things you can do to reduce your stress level is to start learning something new. In a perfect world, it ought to be something new at work. However, that is a bit much. If you're feeling stress at work, taking a night course, or notwithstanding tuning in to books on tape helps set you back in control of your life and, as we've seen, more authority delivers less stress.

Social Support Helps Fight Stress

The last huge thing that you can do to reduce your stress level is to develop a lot of companions to support you. Studies show that, when assembly line workers are permitted to talk and associate at their work stations, their level of stress goes down, and the quality and speed of their work goes up. So also, if you can stroll a few doors down and drop in on a companion for a five-minute discussion, the social contact will start to reduce your anxiety and the stress related to it.

What Does This All Mean for You?

We started with the fluffy reasoning that produces ideas like "good stress," and we learned that stress is intrinsically terrible for you - awful. We found that stress isn't merely in your head - it's making changes in your whole body. What's more, we learned why we have stress in any case - it's an extra reaction to saw danger, that gets activated by current situations like lethal work conditions. What's more, we learned in any event three different ways to reduce your stress level - take more control, start learning new skills and build up a social support network. The primary concern is this: you have to accept position stress genuinely because it can kill you; and there are moves you can make at present, all alone, to start bringing down your stress.

How to Have Clear Thinking

Would you like to have clear thinking at whatever point you need to do it? Here are a few hints to enable you to accomplish it. Try not to imagine that it is difficult. You can think clearly if you attempt to improve yourself. Attempt to do it endlessly.

Go for a stroll. It will help chill off your feeling. After going for a stroll for some time, you will see that your problem will be seen clearly, and you can without much of a stretch settle it. Also, avoid devouring sugar. For what reason would you say you are denied eating sugar? It very well may be demonstrated by one analysis. Attempt to expend sugar at that point, answer math problems. You will see that the problems look progressively confounded. Accordingly, make yourself quieter with specific hints here.

Attempt to show signs of improvement sleep to have clear thinking. The nature of sleep could be accomplished well for having typical brain function at that point attempt to take as much time as necessary for pondering. Unwind and receive a full breath, these exercises help much in improving brain power. Do you know? Better sleep will make you increasingly inventive what's more if you can't think attempt another way like breathing profoundly.

If you need to have clear thinking, never drink alcohol. Take care of business since drinking alcohol gives an awful impact on the effectiveness of the brain, and if you have something to choose, then do what needs to be done. An excessive amount of idea on mind will make individuals get confounded and can't think clearly. At that point, inhale natural air and do work out. These hints are viable enough to make you think clearly.

What Is Logic? What Is Critical Thinking?

Logic is the science of how to evaluate arguments and reasoning. Critical thinking is a process of assessment which uses logic to isolate truth from falsehood, reasonable from unreasonable beliefs. If you need to more readily evaluate the different claims, ideas, and arguments you experience, you need a superior understanding of essential logic and the process of critical thinking.

These are not unimportant interests. They are necessary to using sound judgment and framing rational beliefs about our reality.

Who Cares About Logic?

Is learning about logic and how to appropriately develop arguments critical? A great many people may not need such abilities in their everyday lives, except the truth is that nearly everybody will profit by learning how to think all the more critically.

This does apply to our own beliefs, yet additionally to every one of the ideas and claims that we usually experience. Without the privilege of mental instruments, we have little any expectation of dependably isolating truth from falsehood.

Untalented and Unaware

Everybody commits errors. Frequently, what is most important is the ability to recognize our mistakes initially and after that, what we do about it.

Lamentably, there are fields where the worse an individual is, the more uncertain they are to try and recognize that they have committed errors, substantially less will almost certainly fix them. In reality, they are, in fact, liable to accuse the individuals who know a higher amount of being the ones who aren't right.

Critical thinking and logic are one of these fields. Numerous people envision that they are as of now very excellent at it and hence don't accept that they have to find out additional. This keeps them from consistently improving.

What Is Logic?

People use words like "logic" and "logical" a ton, frequently without truly understanding what they mean.

Carefully, logic is the science or investigation of how to evaluate arguments and reasoning. It is anything but a matter of assessment; it's a science of how discussions must be shaped to be reasonable or right. A superior understanding is critical for helping us a reason and think better. Without it, it's unreasonably simple for us to fall into a mistake.

What Is Critical Thinking?

The expression "critical thinking" is used frequently, yet it isn't in every case, appropriately comprehended. Put permanently, critical thinking means creating trustworthy, regular assessments of an argument or idea.

Critical thinking is a method for isolating truth from falsehood and reasonable from unreasonable beliefs. It as often as possible includes discovering blemishes in the arguments of others. However, that is not all that it's about. It's not just about reprimanding ideas. It is tied in with building up the ability to consider ideas with more noteworthy critical separation.

Understanding and Disagreement

Arguments are about disagreement - people aren't probably going to contend over things they concur on. As obvious as that might be, it isn't generally as visible what, precisely, people disagree on. This is particularly valid for the individuals who are made up for lost time amidst a disagreement.

This is an issue because disagreements can't be settled if those involved don't recognize what their difference is extremely about - or worse yet, really disagree on what they disagree about. If those involved don't work that out, the main thing they'll achieve by contending is to make greater enmity.

Propaganda and Persuasion

Propaganda is any composed, facilitated exertion to persuade masses regarding people to adopt some specific idea, belief, mentality, or perspective.

It's almost effortless to see government propaganda with regards to wartime. The name is likewise material to the endeavors of companies to purchase their items, to defenders attempting to get people to adopt their religion and numerous different circumstances. Understanding the idea of propaganda and how it functions is critical to have the option to contemplate it.

Why is Logic Important?

Why bother to get familiar with logic and arguments? Does it truly make a difference, and does it truly support anybody? Actually, yes it does—and there are a few right motivations to set aside the effort to become familiar with both topics.

Improve the Validity of Your Arguments

The quickest and obvious benefit from such an investigation is that it can enable you to improve the nature of the arguments you use. When you make logically unsound arguments, you are substantially less prone to persuade people that you have a legitimate point to make or get them to concur with you. Regardless of whether they are new to logic, numerous people will realize that there is some problem with some false arguments without being able to identify the deception included.

Abstain from Being Influenced by Others

A moment and firmly related benefit will be an improved ability to evaluate the arguments of others. When you see how cases should be constructed and furthermore how they ought not to be built, you will find a wide range of bad arguments out there. You may even be astounded to find out what bad arguments influence the number of people.

Although you may not realize it promptly, arguments are surrounding us competing for our consideration and acceptance. We hear arguments that we should buy a car an as opposed to car B. We listen to arguments that we should vote in favor of politician Smith instead of for politician Jones. We listen to arguments that we ought to receive this social policy as opposed to that social policy.

In these cases, people are making or ought to be making arguments - and because they are attempting to get you to believe their decisions, you must be able to evaluate those arguments. If you can show that a case is sound and legitimate, not just do you have the motivation to acknowledge it, but you can likewise guard this acceptance at whatever point somebody asks you for what good reason you have done it.

But when you can identify bad arguments, it will be easier for you to liberate yourself from beliefs which are not very much established. It additionally enables you to challenge people making claims which you believe are suspect, but you would otherwise experience issues in clarifying why. That won't generally be simple, because we regularly have an overwhelming passionate and psychological interest in certain beliefs, paying little mind to their validity. Having such apparatuses available to you can guide you in this procedure.

Shockingly, the argument that wins is generally the one who gets said most intense and last, paying little mind to its genuine validity. When it bids to people's feelings, it can even have a better shot of looking unrivaled. But you shouldn't enable others to trick you into believing their claims because they were steady—you need to be able to challenge and scrutinize their affirmations.

Improve Everyday Communication

A further benefit will likewise ideally be an ability to impart all the more evident and viable. The jumbled composition will, in general, originate from muddled thinking, and that this will, in general, arise from a poor comprehension of what an individual is attempting to pass on and why. But when you know how an argument ought to and ought not to be introduced, it will be easier to un-jumble those ideas and change them into a more grounded example.

And keeping in mind that this might be a site managing agnosticism, it is likewise a site which manages skepticism—not only skepticism about religion. Wary request about all topics requires an ability to use logic and argumentation viably. You will have reasonable cause to use such aptitudes with regards to the claims made by politicians and sponsors, not merely religion, because people in those callings submit logical mistakes and fallacies all the time.

Necessarily clarifying the ideas behind logic and arguments isn't sufficient—you need to see and work with genuine examples of the fallacies. That is the reason this book is loaded up with various instances of everything described. Remember that unmistakable, logical composing is just something that will accompany the practice. The more you read, and the more you write, the better you will get - this isn't an attitude that you can get inactively.

Practice Makes Perfect

This present site's discussion is the right spot where you can get such a practice. Not the majority of the composition there is of the most astounding caliber, obviously, and not the majority of the topics will be intriguing or enjoyable. But after some time, you will see some excellent argumentation on a wide assortment of issues. By perusing and partaking, you will have the chance to adopt a considerable amount. Indeed, even the absolute best blurbs, there will promptly recognize that their time in the gathering has improved their abilities to think and write on these issues.

The Importance of Critical Thinking Skills

Critical thinking skills are at an unprecedented low in the US. In broad daylight and private, a large portion of our populace appears to be unequipped for sensibly and insightfully thinking through an issue or problem. What precisely is critical thinking? While meanings of critical thinking can change somewhat, a tremendous essential definition is the ability to use reason, involvement, and knowledge to evaluate and explain an issue. Likewise, to assess the nature of your information and to touch base at an intelligent, sound judgment solution.

Envision, you have a student going to find out about the American Civil War. One teacher tells the student that the war began in 1861 and finished in 1865. The South had slaves. The North didn't. The war was battled to keep the Union together and furthermore to free the slaves. Toward the finish of the war, more than 600,000 thousand men had passed on. The teacher, at that point, tells the student to remember these realities for a test. A different teacher tells a student about the preface paving the way to the war, possibly concentrating on the problem of including free states and slave states to the Union.

Moreover, they may discuss the rights that states had to succeed, and that most countries could never have consented to enter the Union without this ability to leave. This teacher may likewise include that liberating the slaves didn't enter the image until after the war had just begun. At that point in the wake of giving the student this information, and the chance to get more without anyone else, they would advise the student to provide it with a fair, mindful assessment and land at their own decision. The principal teacher is pushing purposeful publicity, and the second is attempting to ingrain critical thinking in the student.

Shockingly our way of life in the US has reproduced a populace that is content with sound nibble news, shallow investigation, and superficial concern. Absence of critical thinking and comprehension of issues usually prompts an effectively lead and controlled populace. An excessive number of people latently acknowledge information being dumped on them with positively no genuine or insightful examination. The alleged Elites are increasingly keen on keeping up power then they are in a specific belief system. That is the reason people of the two sides of the political range need to battle to make beyond any doubt they keep the majority of their Liberties and have free access to information (this does exclude reasonable National Security secrets). Controlling the availability and dispersal of information is the way the gossip elitists keep control and keep up their capacity. This is the reason a constrained government and progressively nearby government is so significant. The less government is associated with people's lives, and the closer it is to home, the more people can influence change. As a consequence, people will use their critical thinking skills all the more regularly and the subsequent keen and reasoned choices will make for a progressively educated and more grounded nation.

CHAPTER TWO

Develop Your Critical Thinking Skills

It's anything but difficult to state, "be progressively skeptical" or "practice better critical thinking," yet precisely how would you approach doing that? Where are you expected to learn critical thinking? Learning skepticism isn't care for learning history—it's not a lot of realities, dates, or ideas. Uncertainty is a process; critical thinking is something you do. The best way to learn skepticism and critical thinking is by doing them... yet, to do them, you need to learn them. How might you break out of this constant circle?

Learn the Basics: Logic, Arguments, Fallacies

Skepticism might be a process. However, it's a process that depends on specific principles about what constitutes excellent and terrible thinking. There's no substitute for the basics, and if you think you know every one of the basics, that is most likely a decent sign that you need to audit them.

Indeed, even experts who work on logic professionally misunderstand things! You don't need to know as much as an expert, yet there are such a large number of different fallacies that can be utilized from multiple points of view that there will undoubtedly be some that you aren't acquainted with, also ways those fallacies can be used that you haven't seen at this point.

Don't expect you know everything; rather, accept you have a long way to go and make it a point to routinely survey the different ways fallacies can be utilized, how logical arguments are developed, etc. Individuals are always finding new ways to mangle arguments; you should stay up to date with what they are stating.

Practice the Basics

It's insufficient to find out about the basics; you need to utilize what you also learn effectively. It resembles finding out about a language in books yet never utilizing it — you'll never find almost equivalent to an individual who works typically on using that language. The more you use logic and the principles of skepticism, the better you'll do it.

Developing logical arguments is one obvious and accommodating way to accomplish this. However, a far better idea might be to assess the arguments of others since this can show you both what to do and what not to do. Your paper's editorial page is an excellent spot to discover the new subject matter. It's the letters to the editor as well as the "proficient" editorials which are regularly loaded up with awful fallacies and essential imperfections. If you can't discover a few mistakes on some random day, you should look all the more carefully.

Reflect: Think About What You're Thinking

If you can come to the heart of the matter where spot fallacies without contemplating it that is extraordinary, however, you can't start not thinking about what you're doing. Quite the opposite truth be told: One of the signs of good critical and skeptical thinking is that the doubter considers intentionally and purposely their thinking, even their critical thinking. That is a general purpose.

Skepticism isn't just about being skeptical of others, yet additionally have the option to prepare that skepticism on your ideas, assessments, tendencies, and ends. To do this, you need to be in the habit of thinking about your contemplations. Here and there, this might be more diligently than learning about logic, yet it produces compensates in a wide range of zones.

In Another words

First, remember that a standout amongst the most crucial parts of serious thinking is evaluating your problem as well as the reliability of your information and its source. Before you can continue with a comprehensive, take a gander at your problem, you need to have trusted and exact information. If possible, a variety of outlets is prescribed to help with perspective.

Next, you will need to address your problem; use intelligence and your experience. Sounds simple, yet this is the place numerous people go off track, not trusting themselves. The vast majority give a lot of trustworthiness to different people's opinions and solutions. Have faith in your innate intelligence and life experiences. Everyone has an inner voice which ought to be trusted.

Try not to be afraid to use different individuals' experiences and input yet think about it while considering other factors and trust your instincts. A noteworthy problem with people developing their critical thinking isn't in hard analysis or meaningful information; it doubts themselves. Sadly, a great many people are insecure with their insight and experiences. If you are more youthful, lean a little bit more towards trusted sources, if you are more established slant more towards your skill and smarts. In the end, be that as it may, depend on yourself, a people innate intelligence, logic, and sound judgment are a lot more grounded than realized.

In conclusion, you will need to continuously chip away at improving your critical thinking with problems big and little. In the long run, your ability will tremendously enhance, resulting in positive impacts on your life. Remember, developing critical thinking skills is like some other skill, the more you work at it, the keener it progresses toward becoming.

Decision Making Basics

An individual ought to adopt a decision making that works for them, as long as it brings out making very much thought out decisions. Every individual builds up a style based on past decisions made and occasions that have happened in his life, and these experiences can either be applicable or accommodating or inhibiting and hurtful. The following are some essential tips that will ideally assist you in your decision-making process:

(1) Only make decisions that are yours to make. There is a big difference between a decision and an opinion. It is essential to comprehend and appreciate the difference,

(2) It is important to remember that, quite frequently, one must decide a series of options or alternatives, none of which might be ideal, that fit the existing circumstances. Making the best possible decision means evaluating information and developing a course of action. It is not necessarily an ethical choice among right and wrong. Regularly, none of the alternatives are

ideal, yet it is commonly important to make a decision based on the best available options.

(3) Avoid making rushed or "snap" decisions, yet besides, avoid the inclination to procrastinate! Leaders should act unmistakably more quickly on less crucial, easily alterable or adaptable decisions, and all the more cautiously or deliberately when determining a course of action with increasingly sweeping ramifications, that will be difficult to change.

(4) Avoid procrastinating. In decision making, timing is frequently critical, and it is no better to make the right decision past the point of no return than to make the wrong decision too soon. Great decision makers strive to make the ideal decision in a timely and applicable way.

(5) Put your ideas and options down on paper. Watch, evaluate, return to the notes, and write your remarks. Use these to help guide making your decision, and to assist you in assuring you've assessed the same number

of available facts and information as accessible and possible.

(6) In considering options, and getting the ideas of others, be mindful so as not to pass judgment on based on who gave you the idea. Numerous terrible decisions have been made because of the decision maker's bias against or for the individual providing the idea or suggestion. Instead, make your decision based on what you believe to be right, and not who you think is right.

(7) Use the "upsides and downsides" technique for evaluating. It organizes you and encourages you to center around the full extent of the matter.

(8) Don't put off making a decision on a littler or increasingly minor point, waiting to determine the bigger picture. Instead, make independent decisions as you come, because it is progressively efficient and practical. You can generally adopt the little points to fit into the decision you prepare for the "big picture," however numerous leaders will in general procrastinate, and become overpowered by the little

spots, in this manner inhibiting decision making on the higher points.

(9) Think about how your decision might impact specific individuals, both positively and negatively. Get the same number of these individuals involved as feasible, because it will both assistance you see the entire issue all the more plainly, yet it will likewise motivate these individuals and encourage an environment of more prominent cooperation and commitment. It is essential to remember that all decisions have ramifications!

(10) It is impossible to predict the future, so regardless of how well you consider your decision, you can't be sure whether it is the right one, or how it will work, with any certainty. Effective leaders and decision makers experience the decision making the process wholly and exhaustively, however ought to never feel they have to apologize if a very much thought out, considered, and the planned idea does not work out just as anticipated.

(11) Think in term of O.O.R. The first "O" is for the objectives you wish to achieve and why you are proceeding; the second "O" is for the options (or alternatives) you feel are available and realistic at the time; and "R" is for the possible ramifications of taking each course of action.

(12) Remember that there is no "rigid" rule for who in an organization should make a decision. While some have theorized that decisions ought to be made at as low a dimension as could be allowed, that is just possible if the organization is the uncommon one that has professionally trained its leadership. Because of the low priority most organizations historically place on professional leadership development and training, it is frequently tricky, from a realistic standpoint, to extensively delegate, and still be confident of getting optimum outcomes.

(13) I have heard leaders state that they have not had the option to decide. Leaders must realize that the very act of not planning ends up being a decision to make no move.

(14) Effective leaders must be allowed to be either right or wrong. In any case, before an organization can follow this rule, it needs to train its leaders sufficiently, and guarantee genuine leaders ascent to leadership positions.

(15) A genuine leader must confide in himself to make the decision and should likewise feel confident that he can deal with anything circumstances, desired or undesirable, follow from there on.

(16) Leaders must evaluate which issues are deserving of spending the time and vitality on to experience this "decision-making process." Effective leaders can't bear to waste time on problems that don't need addressing. Leaders must become familiar with the basics of effective time management.

(17) As numerous alternative courses of action as possible must be evaluated, to have the option to make an informed decision.

(18) Ask, "What might turn out badly? How might I address these worries?" before making a final decision!

(19) It is frequently more comfortable for an effective leader to experience the decision-making process alone, as opposed to as a group exercise.

(20) Remember that piece of the decision-making process is the idea, yet a top to a bottom action plan. It has continuously stunned me what a limited number of organizational leaders enough exploit using an action plan.

(21) Brainstorm and get input to help with accumulating new thoughts and ideas. Be that as it may, it is essential to be selective about who you brainstorm with, because not every person's input is similarly profitable.

(22) Once you've finally made your decision, follow through effectively. Don't "think back" during the implementation stage.

Leaders must realize that somebody will dependably disagree, or need to keep things how they were, or avoid change, or draw out history, and so forth.

Organizations must be continually evolving while maintaining their mission. Organizations that don't will in general stagnate, and organization stagnation, if not tended to, is one of the leading causes of dismal and disappointing outcomes.

Practical Decision Making: Getting It Righter

Until a decision gets made - to adopt an idea, buy something, consent to arrangement terms, choose one thing over another, or make a move in any manner - there can be no complete transaction. With the most exact data, the most productive arrangement, or the absolute best idea or good righteousness, until or except if there are understanding and action, nothing new happens and there is no change. We can be right, intelligent, capable, and moral - and buy-in can evade us paying little mind to how 'right' or 'rational' or essential the new decision would be.

Each decision is a change management problem. Regardless of whether it's a personal decision or the consequence of corporate, scientific, or proficient decisions, a decision speaks to expansion too, or subtraction from, something within the status quo that would be affected by new or different information. So, making a decision isn't merely about the undeniable realities, input/output, risks, uncertainty, or procured information, however about the process of acknowledgment, buy-in, and adaptability of the system to adapt to change.

I understand that a significant part of the decision-making field focuses on 'good data', 'rational decisions', or 'reducing bias', yet the subjective, systemic segment of decision making is regularly discarded: Until or except if there is a route to adoption that is acceptable to the status quo - paying little mind to the efficacy of the outcomes - decision making is incomplete.

GOOD DATA IS NOT ENOUGH

Over and over again, we expect that 'good data' is the lynchpin for 'rational' action. In any case, if that were all that we needed, there'd be significantly less disappointment. How can it happen that even with right on our side we can finish up wrong? By shifting the focus from rational decisions, chances, data, risk, and probabilities - the best outcome - to a focus on enabling our subjective biases to expand the parameters of the hunt, adoption, and possibility, decision making can be progressively compelling.

We've contemplated decision making for centuries, with a predictable focus on a 'rational' outcome dependent on 'facts.' Weighted averages and data/precision appear to be the most utilized organizing principles. We generally, it seems, partner decision making with 'good data' good choices, risk, and assignments to be finished. Daniel Kahneman and Amos Tversky state that individuals make 'casino decisions': they accumulate probabilistic possibilities and figure the best route between them. In any case, following quite a while of experimentation, they found the focus on helping individuals make 'good,' 'rational' decisions to be of "restricted achievement." According to Michael Lewis' new book The Undoing Project, Kahneman said it was essential to assess a decision "not by its outcomes - regardless of whether it ended up being right or wrong - yet by the process that led to it."

I accept the problem lie on the personal, subjective end of decision making. Before we even get to the weighted criteria, data, or 'rational facts,' out to a great extent unconscious belief have confined the range of potential outcomes by limiting our pursuit criteria, restricting our interest and objective setting, and reducing adoption. As such, our process restrains the full range of possibilities. We're not in any case interested about whatever may lie outside the parameters of what we 'know' in our guts, or in our intuition, to be valid. Our unconscious sabotages our decisions. We should shift the focus far from data and the measurably right answer and focus on managing our systemic, subjective bias.

HOW SUBJECTIVE BIAS SABOTAGES US

Give me a chance to explain my shift in focus. As people, we make several small and enormous decisions daily. The more significant part of them are brisk, straightforward, and fluctuate on a continuum among conscious and unconscious: which coat to wear, where to take some time off, regardless of whether to state something or stay silent. When we think something is missing or incomplete and look for a different outcome, we weight and think about facts or givens against our criteria (beliefs, values, history, knowledge, suspicions). All choices get surveyed according to how intently they match our internal, weighted chains of command of beliefs and values (generally unconscious). Indeed, it's just when we're convinced that our present data or status quo appears to be lacking and the new choices feel either progressively exact or agreeable, are we willing to shift our status quo to adopt further information.

Groups or organizations seeking right decisions for new choices accomplish something comparative: facts get inquired about and weighted according to the objectives of a constrained gathering of pioneers and the most acceptable sources; appraisals get made against the status quo and acknowledged industry standards, and change is intended to happen according to some adequate value structure.

Be that as it may, regardless of whether personal or corporate, the human side of decision making is regularly ignored: separate from the facts, the weighting, the 'rational' or the ideal, our subjective biases - sometimes alluded to as our 'intuition', instinct, or our 'gut' - limit what's conceivable. Indeed, well before we determine potential alternatives for choices, we give ourselves over to our unconscious beliefs and subjective biases that make the parameters of possibility in any case. If we don't accept environmental change has a human part, for instance, we won't feel the need to settle on which reuse bin to buy and will find 'rational' reasons not to accept a scientific contention loaded up with demonstrated facts, paying little heed to its efficacy.

WHAT'S OUTSIDE OUR CONSCIOUS CHOICE

Every new decision must comply with our internal equalization, (Systems Congruence): our unconscious, subjective, belief-based criteria are personal, notable, peculiar, and character-based - separate from any outside data accessible or outcome looked for. We even look for references that match our beliefs: with an infinite range of data points available, we just think about that tiny segment of accessible data that sounds good to us, in this manner restricting our data gathering harshly; we reject, ignore, or oppose any incoming data that runs counter to our values and internal status quo. With our individual channels interpreting information, our unconscious biases take in or forget conceivably essential data. If we don't maintain our present beliefs, standards, and status quo we face a conceivably troublesome change in our systemic structure, paying little heed to the facts, or the weighted averages or the 'rational' choice.

Our decisions are confined by our subjective biases and need for Systems Congruence, regardless of whether they are personal decisions or family/business-related ones, whether they lead to 'rational' decisions or not. Indeed, who precisely makes a decision about what's 'rational'? We each consider our decisions 'rational' as they comply with our belief structure and knowledge at the time, we're making them. Imagine saying to yourself, "I think I'll settle on an irrational decision." 'Irrational' is a subjective term utilized by outcasts judging our output against their own beliefs (and what they consider to be 'target' or 'rational' measures). I generally ask, "Irrational according to who?" After all, science is only a story in time, and 'facts' change (Remember when eggs were awful? Or on the other hand when making an online buy was a risk?), and there are quite numerous to choose from!

I once helped a companion settle on how to manage her loft. For a considerable length of time, she battled herself on different sorts of wood and floor plan/design and couldn't shape a decision to make a move on account of her perplexity. When we got to her unconscious weighted chain of command of beliefs, she understood, she detested her home, yet hadn't had any desire to intentionally concede that to herself because moving would evacuate her family. She had unconsciously postponed her decision, deliberately focusing on altogether different issues to abstain from dealing with a lot bigger problem. She was stuck considering the 'wrong' decision criteria for 3 years.

When we ignore our unconscious, we either postpone a decision since it doesn't feel right, assemble data from insufficient sources, utilize halfway data and miss the full picture or possibilities, or face an absence of buy-in, sabotage, or obstruction. To get the right decision, we need to expand our extent of the opportunity and separate ourselves from our biases. We can never get it 'right,' yet we can get it 'righter.'

IS IMPLEMENTATION NECESSARY?

One of my beliefs is that without action, without achieving the yield of a decision, we end up with failure, regardless of the accuracy of the facts. This is quite prevalent in among the Decision Scientist community. After keynoting to 200 Decision Scientists on Facilitating Decision Making a couple of years ago, I sat with them afterword and tuned in to them uproariously bemoan the 97% implementation failure rate (Sadly, a typical problem in the field.) they face. Here was part of our Q&A.

SDM: How would you prepare for a smooth implementation, or encourage buy-in?

We give the best options according to our research. It's their problem if they can't execute. Our main responsibility is to find the correct arrangements and hand them over.

SDM: How would you acquire specific criteria to structure your research?

We speak with folks who want the decision.

SDM: If you're speaking to a subset (influencers, bosses, customers) of users, by what method can buy-in be achieved - even with useful data and rational decisions - if the full set of facts are potentially not being considered? Aren't you limiting your fact-gathering to an inclined subset? Aren't you moving forward without consideration of the individuals who may be involved sooner or later, have unique goals and data, and oppose implementing decisions well outside their value structure?

Not our problem.

SDM: How can say you're offering a 'good decision' if a portion of the individuals who need to use the decision aren't ready, willing, or able to adopt it because their reality was avoided from the initial data gathering?

We gather criteria from the folks who contact us, from perceived sources and weight the probabilities. We give them useful data. Feelings have nothing to do with it. Rational data is objective data.

They wouldn't much think about that by doing initial fact-gathering from as broad a set of individuals involved as conceivable, they'd not just acquire a more comprehensive set of identified goals, parameters and foundational beliefs and values that maintain the status quo, yet they'd set the stage for pursuing on buy-in.

When we use a subset of possibilities and individuals to define the objective criteria for a decision and avoid the available personal standards, and when we use our instinctive decisions as our focal point, we face the possibility of gathering insufficient data and alienating those would might profit by the outcome of the decision; we are ceding control to our emotional, and biased, unconscious. By what method can we willingly take action if it conflicts with our unconscious drivers, regardless of the efficacy of the available information? How might we realize where to gather data from if we seek after a biased section of what's available? How might we know if our decisions will be optimal if we're unconsciously limited by our emotional biases and don't gather data from, perceive, or realize that we are restricting the full set of possibilities?

WHAT DOES OUR UNCONSCIOUS WANT?

All of us pit our unconscious drivers - our beliefs and values, expectations and biases - against our ability to change (And I repeat: any decision is a change management problem. To adopt something new, something old must be replaced or added.). To concentrate only on external facts makes no sense. In request to make our best decisions, we (even teams and families) must integrate our conscious with our unconscious and find a course that expands degree and possibility without provoking resistance. Here are a few questions to ask ourselves:

- What are my gut considerations about what another outcome would resemble, act like, achieve? Am I comfortable with a change? Am I willing to contain/expand the parameters of the status quo? What might cause me to stand up to?

- How far outside of my own beliefs am I willing to go to make beyond any doubt I have as expansive a range of potential data as conceivable? Or on the other hand, should I maintain my present parameters (beliefs, or external mandates) regardless of the confinements this posture on the outcome?

- Would it be advisable for me to add to what I already know? Or on the other hand, am I willing to explore what's outside of my insight base that may make me uncomfortable? Where might I find adequate resources to explore - and what might I find unacceptable?

- What do I have to accept to be happy to consider data that I don't ordinarily trust... and what, accurately establishes trust?

Is there a general idea that's a 'lump up' from my starting place that may encourage expansive consideration? For example, if resistance is apparent, is there an idea, an outcome, which encapsulates the proposed change that doesn't cause resistance? If everyone is fighting over house ownership in a separation, maybe everyone can agree that a house is necessary for everyone's prosperity and push ahead from that point.

STEPS TO BETTER DECISION MAKING

There is a point when gathering data is necessary. In any case, when? Here are steps to knowing when now the right time is:

Make beyond any doubt all users - all - and influencers (or personally, brainstorm yourself for all surrounding data points of possibility, regardless of how outlandish) are involved in the initial data gathering and outcome-setting.

Get internal (personal or team) agreement for abnormal state beliefs, values, and outcomes as to what a final arrangement ought/shouldn't entail.

Inspire concerns, fears, beliefs that any change would bring.

Inspire expectations and viewpoints as to best outcomes, goals, and options.

Everyone involved do research on data sources, consider, comparative ventures, potential problems (or personally, research all brainstormed possibilities) using agreed-upon resources for data gathering, testing, parameters for results.

Reach agreement on 5, at that point begin a typical decision analysis/weighting.

With this approach*, your testing and data gathering will have the possibility of being progressively reliable and complete, will reach the broadest parameters of decision, option, agreement, and will encourage buy-in for action. You'll also be in place for implementing without resistance. Again, the final decision may not be 'correct' because no decisions ever are, yet it will undoubtedly be 'righter.'

Rational Decision-Making Model

A comprehension of cerebral administration will uncover the pastime of managers in tackling hierarchical assets to accomplish the ideal end. Managers are gone up against with challenges and issues that require resolution, and decision practically always. A portion of the problems is minor while others are important to the prosperity of the association, particularly as far as the primary concern and vital execution.

The managerial condition is ending up excessively intricate and dynamic. This requires rational reasoning and rational decision making. Never again will heuristics or rule of the thumb produce any viable solution to hierarchical problems and challenges. Rationality in decision making is never back debatable while irrationality is illogical.

A rational decision-making model is a customary way to deal with understanding decision making. It is optimistic in that it doesn't generally catch the decision-making example of the rehearsing manager yet what ought to establish the managerial decision-making outskirts.

It is frequently alluded to as the rational financial model. It presumes that managers, who are undoubtedly the decision makers, are intelligent and henceforth would dependably engage in an arrangement of steps that will improve the likelihood of achieving the set objectives.

The model endorses a consecutive decision-making process with a stream that incorporates opportunity or problem solution, opportunity or problem recognition, opportunity or problem definition, generation of alternatives, information gathering, evaluation of options, determination of an option, execution of chose alternative and criticism through the assessment of the adequacy or generally of the choice.

Opportunity or problem recognition is vital to powerful decision making. Without opportunity or problem recognition, it might be challenging to characterize the marvel or spot it in a legitimate point of view. Generation of alternative ways to deal with adapting to the circumstance depends to a great extent on how well the condition is characterized.

There is usually a need to accumulate information on the alternatives to find out their attractive quality after an experimental investigation. From there on one choice is chosen after the appropriate screening of the other options. The alternative chose is executed and exposed to facilitate evaluation to furnish criticism that is compared with the first problem.

The problems with this model incorporate shortsighted suppositions that all alternatives will be considered and screened; that exact information will be accessible at no expense, and that decision-makers are rational creatures without hue of emotion and different indecencies which are a piece of their edges.

Regularly than not, managers don't generally engage in rational decision making because of their emotional makeup, level of ability, lack of vital information, oblivious conformity, and time requirements. Subsequently, botches are made, and assets are squandered on "solutions that acknowledge minimal extreme incentive for the association."

Inside limited attentiveness, I think about the model a compelling one for a reception in my association. It will fill in as a manual for line managers and expert framework to creating solutions to problem dependent on rational considering negative emotion and rule of the thumbs which have all the earmarks of being the rule that particular case.

The entire thought is to give them a system to observational problem fathoming. Anyway, it is essential that preparation is led for them, particularly in the zone of problem recognition, thoughts generation, and evaluation.

CHAPTER THREE

What is Your Mental Model?

There are numerous purposes behind clash, yet they eventually can be refined into the way that we as a whole have diverse mental models of how the world works. These mental models are both useful and frightful. From one perspective, they are unbelievably helpful in the way that they disentangle our lives and spare us the vitality of reexamining every viewpoint we have each time we are gone up against with a circumstance.

These models are on the whole relevant. We have various models for every feature of life, from who we choose to be friends with, to what sort of music we tune in to, to the kinds of nourishment we eat and the make of vehicle we drive.

Your parameters and mental model for restaurant selection may be that the restaurant use just privately developed produce and have a veggie lover selection at sensible costs virtually. Your friend may have a mental model that directs they dine in higher-end restaurants that have the best wines and choicest cuts of meat. These are the furthest edges of the range, and there likely isn't a lot of a trade-off for the general population at either end in finding a spot they can dine together (for example the money related perspective alone is generally a deal breaker if nor is eager to move).

Or on the other hand, take, for instance, your decision in where you live. One individual needs to live in a metropolitan zone encompassed by movement, shops, theater, restaurants, displays, and assorted variety and their accomplice needs to live in a rural or community atmosphere where there is grass in the middle of the houses and one stop sign around the local area.

We donate truly see deliberately that these mental models are in real life until we face somebody who has contradicting mental models. If you are among similar individuals in a detached atmosphere, you can stay away from the information of correctly understanding different models of the world are conceivable. It's not that you don't understand these different convictions are out there, nonetheless, because you know contrasts of confidence are out there at any rate as per TV, motion pictures, and the web.

Issue emerge when we are not aware of our mental models. We can stall out and be obstinate and think our own is the primary way. I've witnessed this with more established people in my family - there's a correct way and an incorrect way, and that is how it is. Enough said. They believe that there is just a single way for the world to work, and the issues of the world lay in the resistance of everybody who doesn't share their world view.

That would be a fantastically substantial weight, to be the attendant of the truth concerning how the world works. How does this fit into influence? Indeed, this falls under the heading of knowing thyself. When we reveal our mental models, we can reverse engineer where things aren't working, or if they are working, we can reverse engineer to perceive how we've turned out to be so fruitful at what we show.

My supervisor never tunes in to anything I need to state. He'll request my supposition at that point do precisely what he intended to in any case. Why trouble?"

"My employees don't generally think much about their work. The main thing that appears to rouse them is the week's end. Speculation I'll need to do it without anyone's help."

Sound well-known? Those are two different views of a similar situation. They are mental models in real life, and they strengthen a negative example of behavior that is at last ruinous to an organization from multiple points of view.

What are the mental models?

Mental models are profoundly imbued assumptions or generalizations that influence how we comprehend the world and how we make a move. Some different words we use for mental models are viewpoints, beliefs, assumptions, and outlook, to give some examples. Mental models are regularly the best barriers to implementing new ideas in organizations. However, they are additionally the zone of organizational learning where organizations can make the most significant effect.

Tragically, assumptions, the word regularly used to allude to mental models, have a negative meaning to the vast majority of us. We've all heard the familiar maxim, "You realize what happens when you accept? It makes an ___ out of you and me." Well, you can fill in the clear. Assumptions, in any case, are the main way we can make feeling of our mind-boggling world. It is beyond the realm of imagination to expect to have complete information about each situation we experience, so by their very nature, our assumptions or mental models are fragmented and subsequently imperfect. Generally, be that as it may, our mental models work well for us.

There are those events, then again, where our mental models lead us adrift. An extraordinary example of how flawed mental models can originate from the old anecdote of the blind men and the elephant, where a few blind men are feeling different parts of an elephant and depicting it. The portrayals without anyone else's input are inaccurate, yet when consolidated into one, give a more explicit but still imperfect depiction of what an elephant indeed resembles. Mental models resemble puzzle pieces that we need to fit together into a bigger entirety. As different mental models are recognized, another part falls into place, and we see a clearer picture, yet in this work, we don't have the highest point of the puzzle box to direct us. We should grab along like the blind men.

Mental models influence what we find in situations and make strengthening examples of behavior. In the case given toward the beginning of this article, the employee sees an overbearing and controlling manager, while the manager sees employees who need to put in the base. Accordingly, the employees become disengaged, and the manager attempts to micromanage more - not a beneficial situation in any organization. The more the manager attempts to control the case, the more disengaged the employees become, bringing about a contrarily strengthening cycle. The visible part of the period, the behaviors, increases the undetectable part, the beliefs, or mental models.

What skills do individuals need to create?

So how can one break out of this descending winding? The initial step is to recognize the gap between what we accept to be valid and what is, in reality, evident, or to put it all the more precisely, the difference between mental models and current reality. There are two principal zones of skills in which individuals can practice working with mental models: 1) skills of reflection and 2) skills of inquiry.

Skills of reflection include hindering our thinking with the goal that we become progressively mindful of how we structure our mental models and how they influence our behavior. We can do this in a few ways. One way is to turn out to be increasingly mindful of perceiving when we make what is regularly alluded to as "jumps of abstraction," that is mentioning generalizations based on our objective facts without any data to back it up. In the manager-employee example, the employee watches the manager requesting a supposition yet then not acting upon it. The employee at that point hops to the end that the trough truly isn't keen on subordinates' ideas. Thus, the manager watches disengagement and presumes that it must be because the employees don't generally think about their work. One way to keep away from this entanglement is to pose the inquiries:

- "What is the data on which my beliefs or generalizations are based?"
- "Have I at any point seen any disconfirming evidence to my beliefs?"
- "Am I willing to think about how conceivable it is that my beliefs might be inaccurate?"

Another strategy for developing skills of reflection is frequently alluded to as uncovering the "left-hand column." The "left-hand column" speaks to thoughts we regularly have during discussions yet don't well-spoken. By really writing these thoughts down afterward, we are making our mental models unmistakable. For example, the manager who views his employees as unengaged may assemble a conference of his department to report another vital heading for his group. In the wake of exhibiting the idea, he requests reaction and is met with stony quiet. His quick view might be, "Man! What is it going to take to light a fire under these individuals?" If an employee reacts with lukewarm help, he may likewise think, "Goodness holy cow! Here we go with the lip administration once more! Wouldn't they be able to have an independent mind?" Each of these reactions fortifies the manager's mental model yet writing them down makes it workable for him to separate himself enough from the belief to begin to recognize it for what it is, a generalization.

The last strategy for developing skills of reflection is to recognize the gap between what we state we accept, our embraced hypothesis, and what we do, our theory being used. Put another way; we should begin contrasting our words with our actions or behaviors. Utilizing the manager-employee example once more, the manager may accept that essential participative leadership makes a beneficial group, yet his practice isn't sending that message to his employees. Until he recognizes that gap, no learning or change can happen.

Skills of inquiry shape how we work in up close and personal interactions. When we have started to practice our skills of reflection, we would then be able to begin to surface and examine our mental models with others. In doing as such, we should recall that our mental models are just pieces to the puzzle. In the Skilled Facilitator, Roger Schwarz has built up a strategy called the mutual learning model that can enable individuals to sharpen their relational skills. It is based on the assumptions that everyone sees things differently, and it is those differences that make open doors for learning and innovativeness. It is likewise based on the belief that everyone is acting with respectability. One can practice the mutual learning model by:

- Testing your assumptions by articulating them and requesting affirming or disconfirming evidence;
- Sharing all significant information: retaining information will prompt a less complete picture;
- Being straightforward by putting your thinking on the table as opposed to your completed idea;
- Concentrating on interests, not positions, that is, discussing and consenting to results before hopping to arrangements;
- Talking about those thoughts in the "left-hand column" that are regularly driving your actions;

- Offsetting backing with an inquiry that is, getting some information about different points of view as much as you clarify your own.

These skills, in blend with the powers of reflection, will release the ability to change mental models and to begin pushing the organization toward supportable change. To improve our behavior, we should initially change the beliefs after that those behaviors are based.

In what capacity would organizations be able to change mental models from barrier to use point?

Working with mental models is the most challenging place to begin constructing a learning organization yet can yield the best measure of change. Developing and molding mental models means changing both individual and organizational behavior - a difficult task, best case scenario. It is a procedure that requires tolerance and diligence. The accompanying conditions will enable organizations to diminish the barriers to surfacing and inspecting mental models:

- Make a sheltered environment wherein employees feel right surfacing and analyzing their mental models; it should likewise be an environment where choices are based on what's best for the organization, not on legislative issues;
- Help your employees build up their skills of reflection and inquiry;
- Advance decent variety as opposed to similarity;
- Settle on a truce; everyone does not need to concur with the different mental models that exist; everyone is only an extra piece of information;
- Be OK with vulnerability; we will never know the whole story.

This procedure requires individuals and organizations alike to change how they consider the nature of work. When those barriers are decreased, an organization can begin to see mental models become influence points for advancement. Those negative fortifying circles change into upward spirals of accomplishment.

Are Your Mental Models on the High or Low Road?

Diminish Senge, in his "The Fifth Discipline: The Art and Practice of The Learning Organization" (1990), describes mental models as "profoundly ingrained assumptions, generalizations, or even pictures of images that influence how we comprehend the world and how we make a move." Mental models have a significant impact on how we view, respond to, and react to the world; they shape our decisions, relationships, and quality-of-life. They influence us on all dimensions - individual, social, professional, organizational, national, and worldwide.

My purpose is to raise your dimension of familiarity with what mental models are and how they operate. Practical neuroscience principles and devices help you challenge, change, and deal with your mental models for a superior, more serene, and less unpleasant life.

Individual Observations

- Mental models have stored information and emotional imprints of how your brain perceived and recollected direct close to home experiences, just as information learned from a third gathering or indirect source like the media.

- Models that yield harmful outcomes to you as well as others are good candidates for examination and changed thinking.

- Formed after some time from gathered information; they may likewise be grown quickly and profoundly depending on their importance and emotional impact.

- Most people are ignorant of their models, where they originated from and their belongings.

- They are unobtrusive and challenging to identify and describe.

- They appear to operate in a "back room" or subconscious piece of our brain.

- Our models will, in general, get stronger after some time as human instinct needs to be "right" about its opinions.
- They could conceivably be verifiable through direct experience or independent observations from integral people.

I believe the core question is "the way well do my mental models serve me and others," instead of "are my mental models right or wrong?" There is no right way of taking in and processing sensory information since everybody perceives and interprets information differently. A group of people agreeing on something doesn't make it true; the procedure only bonds the group around something they hold to be true. Unnecessary contentions and even wars result because of differences of opinion about mental models.

Evaluating

This regular day to day existence situations gives you a grip of what mental models resemble; each pair contains differences of mindset for illustrative purposes. As you look them over, ask yourself which ones might serve you and others best, as opposed to deciding on what might be correct or in error. The purpose of this exercise is to shift your focus to a "high road" or positive perspective for evaluating mental models. Ideally, these precedents will stimulate your thinking to write down the mental models that serve you well or poorly.

Low Road: Good ideas for innovation are drying up, and there is limited opportunity for me to thrive.

High Road: Good ideas for new items, innovation, and services are perpetual and infinite.

_____

Low Road: We live in a competitive world of scarcity.

High Road: We live in a world of limitless opportunity where situational cooperation is possible.

Low Road: Girls do poorly in math and science.

High Road: Anyone can learn what interests him or her, when in a supportive environment.

Low Road: You can't confide in people who look, act, and talk a certain way.

High Road: There are trustworthy and untrustworthy people in varying backgrounds.

Low Road: In this economy, nobody will interview me, substantially less, hire me.

High Road: I have transferable skills and positive traits that some business is looking for.

Low Road: I can't confide in myself in the driver's seat because of my driving record and what my companion says.

High Road: A refresher course will make me a more secure, more reliable, and better defensive driver.

Low Road: I can't learn new things since I made reduced levels, and my educator said I was stupid.

High Road: My brain has an infinite capacity to develop, get stronger, learn quickly, and make incredible decisions.

Low Road: It's unlikely I'll live past 73 as a result of my family health history.

High Road: Good health practices and a positive mental attitude will increase my quality-of-life and maybe add a very long time to my life span.

In conclusion, mental models are what we believe and hold to be true about life. They are our "software programming" that drives thinking, opinions, and behaviors. There is always an outcome from each mental model, although they may not be visible. People eagerly concur or disagree on the reality of their mental models. The defining minute for challenging a mental model happens when the focus shifts to the desired outcome. Clarity can best be achieved by examining holes between what is desired and the result that happens. This is the leading way I know to break the perpetual cycle of defending and attacking mental models.

Meditation is the process of understanding ones possess the mind, intending to follow your very own Thought Chains to create a usable Mental Model.

Our minds are dynamic always. As we interact with our environment, our minds are still making thought chains. This prompts an endless torrent of commotion. It resembles having a radio station, set to a similar channel, playing in your mind for endlessness. Without the advantage of volume control or an on-off switch, you are genuinely lost. Yoga and Meditation give you volume control and an on-off switch to utilize at whatever point you have to.

The majority of our thoughts and actions are created from these mental thought chains. We are what we think. So, then it pursues that we ought to consider understanding how the mind works, understanding how our own minds function, as something critical, and to be paid attention to very.

It bears rehashing. This is the thing that Meditation does. It is a process that depends on a working model of how our minds work. Meditation is a process that enables us to get ourselves. Through Meditation you can;

o Look at your very own thoughts,
o Look at your thoughts from the viewpoint of the observer and the observed,
o Learn how to change the way you think, to be increasingly beneficial,
o Realize that the way you think and interact with the world, decides how happy or miserable you are, lastly,
o Realize the numerous physical and mental advantages that yoga and Meditation gives.

Mental movement creates thoughts that relate to different thoughts. So, for instance:

- ❖ You see somebody that reminds you of an old friend named Bob,
- ❖ You think," I genuinely like Bob,"
- ❖ You wonder what Bob is doing,
- ❖ You wonder how the old gang is getting along,
- ❖ You wonder if Bob is on Facebook,
- ❖ You proceed to look at Facebook, to locate your old friend Bob and most of your other old friends from the gang.

So the underlying interaction with the environment triggers a specific action. This usually is the situation. First, you react to the person that reminds you of Bob. You respond to the outside environmental improvement. You, the observer, at that point, proceed to observe the boost and react. This action triggers one more thought and perception and reaction, and one more and again.

You may even create thought chains that will, in the long run, lead to a shocking thought example or subject matter. For instance:

- ✓ You begin seeing the person that reminds you of Bob,
- ✓ You observe that you "like" Bob,
- ✓ Bob makes you feel good,
- ✓ You think, "Bob was always fit as a fiddle, he always practiced a ton,"
- ✓ You consider you possess physical molding,
- ✓ You observe that you aren't especially happy about the shape that you are in,
- ✓ This makes you feel bad,
- ✓ You think, "I need to get to the exercise center and workout harder."
- ✓ You at that point observe, this makes you feel good, yet you genuinely don't have room schedule-wise to get to the rec center today since you need to work late,

✓ You at that point observe that you feel ineffective that you won't almost certainly work out this evening.

In the above thought chain, you went off subject, and you may have seen, that you went from feeling good to feeling bad to feeling good, to feeling bad once more, all inside a couple of minutes. Yowser! Insane right.

However, this is actually what we always do. We continually subject ourselves to this unbeneficial mental move. We are moving to start with one chain of thoughts then onto the next, regularly without monitoring what's occurring us.

You have no clue how to stop it, change it, or if nothing else not to have it negatively influence you. Sometimes you'll even carry on without acknowledging what you're doing.

Through Yoga and Meditation, you will figure out how to screen your rational thought chains and perceive ineffective mechanical examples in your reasoning. You will frame a working model of how your mind functions, with the goal that you can without much of a stretch, see negative thought chains and start to create new, positive thoughts to supplant them. You will push ahead with your life and manifest a fulfilling and lively reality.

CHAPTER FOUR

Mental Models: The Box Everyone Is Trying to Think Outside of

How often week after week completes a businessperson here, "It's an ideal opportunity to do some outside box thinking?" Mental models are the box everybody is attempting to get away. Mental models prevent thinking forward events. Personal manners of thinking are constructed through observation, creative mind, and cognizance of the world. A person sees a candy bar and is confident it is a candy bar, or is it a cell phone with a candy bar case? The imaginative cell phone case was a helpful thinking forward event since it deconstructed a mental model. The undeniable utilization of mental models is to a person's perspective on her or himself in connection to the environment. Self-idea is constructed through apparent abilities, social assignments, and training. Quite a bit of this self-idea prompts intuitive assumptions.

Human assumptions spill over into business. Most businesses flourish with remaining in front of the competition and comprehend that when lack of concern sets in, the upper hand will be lost. Business leader assumptions lead to comfort, which simplifies the real world. Often these assumptions render organizations stuck in a similar spot as innovation cruises them by. Huge multi-channel corporations are mainly influenced by this wonder as representatives and the executives become increasingly more incoherent from the more prominent corporate mission. Cross-grid worldwide organizations specifically have a notoriety for having turned out to be agreeable. "This is the way it's always been done," is expressed again and again as organizations lose a piece of the pie to concealed competition and innovation.

The narrative of the large company that overlooks groundbreaking events and is in this manner undermined by the little, yet agile, the contender is told again and again in business colleges. The solution for childish assumptions is a portion of the outside box thinking. Outside box thinking can make the most prominent organizations deft in their necessary leadership. People are characteristically imperfect and need support foreseeing future business trends because of assumptive mental models. The picture of competition around a company, which workers build, is just a model. A reasonable decision for any company is the option of picking outside box thinking as assurance against lack of concern, brand equity loss, and client whittling down.

Try not to Wait Until You Need Corporate Emergency Triage.

In some cases, the most out-of-the-box thing a company can do is search outside for assistance to develop a superior kind of different. Outside the company, however outside the industry. As much as your company or association needs an innovation consultant, you likewise need one that comprehends weightiness as an establishment and venturing stone, not an idea in retrospect.

Each industry and company have its own culture, and that culture often delivers a kind of "customary target blindness." Similar thoughts keep coming up because the same individuals are entrusted with coming up with new answers for old issues. Eventually, a company either enhances its way to the highest point of the industry, or it stagnates its way into liquidation.

When Is Positive Thinking Actually Negative?

Also, what are the means you can take to rehearse solid, adjusted, positive thinking?

If you're a positive thinker, I'm not catching that's meaning, precisely? Does being positive propose that you will engage positive thoughts? How might you be able to do that perhaps? A few people attempt, ineffectively, to do so. The explanation behind their difficulty in keeping up an alleged positive viewpoint is self-evident.

Every day, a constant number of problems happen, and those problems demand solutions. In any case, to discover solutions, you need to consider the issues, and that appears to raise a contention in people whose objective is to be altogether positive. You can't know about the requirement for a solution except if you're additionally aware of the problem. So except if you are evading all issues of any sort, you'll reasonably need to consider problems regularly.

If it's a good judgment that to discover a solution you need to take a gander at the problem, at that point where did the idea originate from that you should notice the positive? It might arise from a particularly American idealistic propensity. It merits investigating how this attitude - that the sky is the limit if you're positive enough wound up both an advantage and an obligation that influences would-be positive thinkers all over.

This can-do spirit, when used fittingly, is related to the certainty that gives you a chance to push ahead, notwithstanding all evident limitations. This can be a brilliant resource, at any rate when it gives you the solidarity to push forward amid obviously testing conditions. Such positive attitudes have helped imaginative thinkers attempt hard tasks that had never been attempted, and have yielded incredible developments, new styles of craftsmanship, new organizations, and advancements of various types.

It's a disgrace this bright side of positive thinking has turned out to be so enticing to such a significant number of people - they neglect to see the limitations that frequently surface when you're solely observing just the significant parts of everything.

It's calming to consider the shadow side of the can-do spirit. Consider the instance of a company like Enron that would not find problems that their informants were cautioning about. This can-do spirit, when joined with self-fancy, put the company stuck in an unfortunate situation since they were so loaded with their positive sight-seeing that they considered themselves as past the need to tune in to the warnings. Instead, they attempted to escape into their positive cloud of self-important deceptive suspicions about the real world.

How a chipper pop song urges you to be in Denial

The ability to deny problems is unequivocally communicated in the favorite Johnny Mercer lyrics of the Harold Arlen song, Accentuate the Positive. It was composed after Johnny Mercer went to a sermon by Father Divine, who concentrated on the idea of eliminating the negative in your thinking and focus on the positive. With regards to a speech, such plans can be helpful and motivating.

You go to a sermon to be lifted, inspired, and offered would like to confront the up and coming week. Furthermore, to the individuals who were buried in the dark cloud of their pessimism, that message was presumably ideal for overwhelming those substantial clouds. Sermons have an essential reason, and they likewise have their limitations when their sincerely charged energy is substituted for consistent discernment.

Assume that you do turn out to be entirely positive? When you become inspired enough to escape your dark cloud, what happens when you shift to just giving yourself a chance to think upbeat and confident thoughts? There is a particular limitation with attempting to cover over problems with only positive thoughts. The cheerful talk makes you feel better for a minute, yet it won't fix your problems - they're still there. Except if you start taking a gander at the situation and analyzing potential solutions, nothing will change.

When you take a gander at the lyrics of the Accentuate The Positive song, the desire towards Denial is made plain, since you are asked to eliminate the negative. Presently that appears, at first, to be a suggestion to keep away from misery. Also, ideally, perhaps that is the thing that the song should mean. If the song were proposing that you can figure out how to be positive enough to consider inventive solutions to your problems, this would be helpful.

Lamentably, you can take the lyrics another way - as a suggestion to abstain from referencing or thinking about problems. Numerous people make significance in merely along these lines. Notice that following the idea that you accentuate the positive, you are encouraged to eliminate the negative. Indeed, in what capacity will you translate that suggestion? Ideally, you would reduce the propensity to surrender - you would transcend miserable attitudes. Appropriately comprehended, you would change your negative propensity for thinking, and start searching for sensible solutions to your situation.

In any case, numerous people take this line of the song, about eliminating the negative, as a suggestion to not try thinking about issues, or managing problems by any stretch of the imagination. Such people will, in general, say that they are attempting to remain positive. That frequently implies that they don't have any desire to take a gander at problems by any means - otherwise called evasion and Denial. Such reluctance to effectively discover solutions through genuine evaluation, while putting a gleam of a positive turn on everything, really prompts a downward winding of debilitation.

How well-intended metaphysical teachings add to denial, despair, and debilitation

Metaphysical teachings appear to have added to this tendency towards denial, through oversimplified teachings about the intensity of resonance. You may have heard that everything in the universe functions through resonance, where everything is contrasted with tuning forks that resonate with one another. Notice how this honest conviction, attempting to take a principle of material science, and use it as metaphysical teaching, drives numerous people into the state of denial.

To start with, you are told that everything is resonating like a tuning fork. At that point, you are assured that your positive contemplations are resonating with all the positive powers in the universe. And after that, you are advised that your negative considerations will resonate with all the negative influences in the world.

By what means will you interpret that understanding? Everything begins to sound genuine and foreboding, and it brings up an unreasonable fear about discussing problems by any means - all things considered, they're negative, aren't they? When you fear something, you attempt to avoid it. You may come to accept that looking at problems, or discussing concerns, is some way or another amplifying a negative reality that will exacerbate the situation.

Over and over again, the metaphysical teachings leave you with a cutting-edge adaptation of the old era fear of the fiend. Then still, actually now the advanced fear is that if you take a gander at a problem or discussion about concerns and issues in the world, that is by one way or another Negative and Bad, and should along these lines be avoided altogether.

If just metaphysical teachings shared the excellent points of how to use resonance in a decent engaging way, that would be fine. They, by and large, don't. Instead, they give the ingredients to fear and denial, where everyone needs to concur that everything is beautiful and that everything is mystically getting better.

This used to be called sweeping things under the rug, and with radical positive thinking, that irregularity in the carpet gets bigger and bigger.

There are whole gatherings of metaphysical understudies who think it sensible to react in discussion with real understanding. They imagine themselves as contributing to a positive universe and consider every to be and strong statement as co-creating an ever-better world. If just it were so straightforward - you could certify your way to continual accomplishment in life, in a positive upward winding of continually flawless improvement - with never notice about any problems.

Deplorably, this tendency to cover it over with upbeat talk prompts something contrary to happiness, since you feel step by step separated from the real world and detached from helpful solutions.

Possibly this reminds you of the well-known adage, that if you don't have something pleasant to state, at that point don't utter a word by any stretch of the imagination. Sounds suspicious like disempowering denial. Does anything improve through this avoidance, or does a stuck situation remain stuck?

The ever-positive style of probability thinking has spilled into the business world, wherein the playful, continually positive individual is considered as supportive to the business, and the representative who scrutinizes the problems, or goes about as an informant, is considered as a troublemaker to be disregarded. Yes, there is a spot for the playful character, however positive spin and the can-do spirit can never supplant consistent discernment. What's more, how about we see that state - unwavering judgment - for a minute.

Why neutrality and clarity have been wrongly decided as less compelling than advertised up glad thinking

Clarity is neutral, which is neither positive nor negative. What's more, without clarity, you are either dazzled by the haze of real confident sparkle in your mind or brought down by the overwhelming tides of despair. So, this fear of misery is by one way or another associated with the self-dazzled condition of puffed-up positive thinking.

Might it be able to be that the individuals who dogmatically insist that everyone should be positive consistently are harboring despair?

No wonder they must be so positive always - they fear that they will sink into a negative state. Furthermore, they will, as well, since they haven't found the middle way - the state of clarity - the way that rises above positive and negative thinking. Neutrality and transparency are neither positive nor negative. Thus, this liberates you to see your problems in a quiet, composed way.

Where in current thinking is the missing neutrality - the needed clarity? For some odd reason, it appears in the Johnny Mercer lyrics. In the wake of being told to highlight the positive, and in the wake of being encouraged to eliminate the negative, you are cautioned not to disturb Mr. In-between. Ok ha - it appears that Mr. In-between is the code word for that neutral state of mind that is neither positive nor negative.

Be that as it may, is it genuine what the tune says - that you should eliminate the in-between state? No wonder people think that they need to avoid that feared in-between state - the domain of Mr. In-between - with the goal that they can enter the high place that is known for the glittering positive state of mind.

Be that as it may, you weren't told about the beautiful, supportive parts of in-between thinking, would you say you were?

Regardless of whether in a spiritual message, or another age class, or a business seminar, you were given the reasonable decision to be either positive or negative. That isn't reasonable for you, because most states of consciousness aren't positive or negative - and they should be. For what reason is that?

Go past the cutoff points of presumptuous, guileless thinking.

When you take a gander at a problem, you need to consider numerous potential outcomes for what the reason or reasons for the situation might be. You need neutral clarity for that.

When you think about potential solutions for the situation, you need to have the option to verify those different solutions. You need to have the opportunity to consider the answers with the clarity of mind that gives you a chance to perceive whether the answers are proper and doable. Again, you require neutral clarity - Mr. In-between.

What happens when you overlook your neutral clarity?

Notice how when you supplant your neutral clarity with oversimplified positive thinking, your ability to scrutinize solutions winds up limited - because every one of the solutions looks incredible. Every thought is virtuoso - Not.

In like manner, when you stall out in negative, sad thinking, your ability to find solutions is limited - because there is no room in the mind to think about solutions by any stretch of the imagination.

In any case, is there any good reason why positive shouldn't think consequently give you the solutions - all things considered, aren't positive energies expected to lead a positive way unavoidably?

The reason that positive thinking ends up contrary is easy to comprehend when you examine it for a moment. Positive thinking assumes that something is good, only because you give it certainty and conviction. What's more, in real life, not all decisions produce desirable outcomes - and some can be hazardous. Positive thinking assumes that everything will work. In real life, that isn't so. Positive thinking believes that any decision went into in a positive temper, will undoubtedly be valuable. This isn't valid.

Does this imply that if you let go of being positive all the time that you're abandoning positive thinking? Not in any way - you're renouncing extremism. You're leaving denying your common sense. You're abandoning denying your insight. You're relinquishing the positive thinking extremism that denies your entitlement to serenely find the solutions that are accessible to you - when you are eager to access them.

So what is the correct spot for the can-do spirit - the sky is the limit mentality - the nothing-will-stop-us feeling? These are altogether designed to uplift your senses. When you need a passionate lift, utilize these positive frames of mind and sentiments to lift yourself out of the bogs of sadness. In any case, never accept that positive thinking is going to give you wisdom, common sense, or clear answers - it's not designed to do that.

Appropriately utilized, positive thinking clears the spider webs clear, and advises you that solutions are conceivable - however at that point, you will need impartial clarity to push ahead viably.

You need to have the option to use positive thinking carefully, and you need to have the opportunity to utilize it for its planned reason - to shield you from stalling out. Be that as it may, if you let yourself get bolted into happy-talk land, where no issues exist, and where all solutions are similarly right, at that point your condition is possibly marginally superior to anything when you were stuck in negative thinking.

Guided contemplation

This causes you to access viable solutions with wisdom, clarity, and elegance:

1. Take a gander at a situation that worries you.

2. Imagine that you contain that situation in its very own bubble of vitality. This gives you a touch of sound separation and lets you stay steady and focused.

3. Here's the place you get the opportunity to be positive - disclose to yourself that there are solutions for this situation. Don't begin thinking about what they may be only yet - necessarily realize that solutions can be found. That's real positive thinking.

4. Presently put your positive thinking that aside for a moment and put on your clear-thinking neutrality hat. Imagine that you can take a gander at the situation with a clear-thinking set of x-ray spectacles so that you can search inside the case - regardless you're wearing your bright thinking neutrality hat.

5. Take a gander at the obvious solutions. Don't concur with them. Write them down. Obvious answers are the solutions that anybody would think of. Simply think about them, yet don't line up with them yet.

6. Presently think about the creative solutions. Write them down in a rundown, regardless of whether they appear to be doubtful, awkward, weird, or not regular solutions. Don't concur with them, and get them recorded.

7. Presently you're going to investigate every conceivable solution - the obvious ones, and the creative ones. Wear your clear-thinking neutrality hat.

8. When you take a gander at every solution, put that solution in a bubble of light. This keeps it in its little universe and shields you from getting excessively connected to it. Along these lines, think about the apparent solutions and creative solutions. Write any experiences you have about these.

9. Investigate your notes. Regardless you're wearing your bright thinking that. If any of the solutions appear to be unseemly, cross them out of your rundown.

10. Take a gander at the potential solutions. While as yet remaining genuinely unbiased, have somewhat of a creative conceptualize with the ideas. Get a sense about

which solutions are doable. Since if you'd like to join any of the answers.

11. In the coming days, explore - in a reasonable, grounded way - the ideas that appear to be generally valuable.

12. If you end up getting into the foreboding shadow state, put on your positive thinking hat, and advise yourself that solutions are certainly accessible - when you access them.

13. Also, more often than not, you'll be wearing your clear thinking, neutrality hat. That's since you need to have a clear awareness of what's going on, so you can push ahead cleverly.

Clarity and neutrality - the exciting new stars of higher awareness

If this idea of being clear-headed and unbiased sounds exhausting, reconsider. Clarity resembles turning up the magnifying focal point on a magic microscope or telescope - you can see the excellence of the sky, or the more profound reality of anything you examine, with exquisite clarity. Neutrality gives you a chance to be thoroughly present. It's what the old sages were talking about when they guided you to leave your waking dream. They were always instructing you to wake up, and now you know what that means.

Perhaps it jumps out at you that you can be positive and clear-headed in the meantime. You can. The explanation behind recommending that you put your positive that aside for a time was so you could get acquainted with neutrality and find out about what it can instruct you. Positive expectations are fine and dandy, yet when they meddle with your capacity to have a clear sense of things, at that point, you're enjoying something that is never again positive - ungrounded dream or refusal.

Presently you realize that you don't need to puff yourself up with ceaselessly positive happy talk. In any case, are there excessively negative people? They are the people who demand that there are no potential solutions and that you need to accept life as it comes to you since everything is pointless. That's detached, sad, and negative. Don't stall out there, either.

You aren't one of those negative people. Almost sure, you're perusing this since you'd like to be increasingly positive, yet you had doubts about whether positive thinking was the straightforward solution it's sometimes professed to be. Furthermore, presently, you realize that you can be positive in a sound adjusted way since you have the means of being keenly and reasonably positive.

There is curious equality about the universe of positive thinkers and negative thinkers. The natural waking dream of the negative thinkers, encompassed by their negative, sad mists, isn't so different from the consistently positive thinkers who are puffed up with ceaseless happy talk. The two sorts of people are stuck in a restricted, waking dream that keeps them from the rich profundity and clarity that life offers in every moment.

When you explore any situation without sugar-covering it with advertised up positives, you have the means to stand up to the location and find creative solutions that really can improve your life.

Your life is unendingly enjoyable - not because you're siphoned up with happy bubbles - but since being available puts you in the unparalleled view of the best occasion - your very own life. When you're available in every moment of your life, and you experience it with clarity, you realize that there is something more significant than stunning joy, and more satisfying than a foggy trust in a marvelous dream future.

How to Simplify Thinking and Everything

We as a whole face the difficulties in life, particularly when we should consider instead mostly tolerating. We ask: Can we simplify our life? Would we be able to discover a straightforward concept that is adequate for analyzing, overseeing, and developing anything and everything? Would we be able to take care of any issue or win any challenge utilizing a straightforward concept? Have you at any point thought about whether we could diminish everything to one idea?

With these inquiries, I spent the most recent couple of years, analyzing our thinking, and our social and financial circumstances. Through observing my very own thinking, talking about with people their issues, and examining the formal rationale and brain science, I found the accompanying ideas worth sharing.

For any business of life, my point of view is that each activity is based on some common points. If we can comprehend those common points present in any activity, we can dodge slip-ups and make achievement sure. Be that as it may, what is implied by these common points? I will attempt to clarify quickly.

If anything, individual, gathering, time, space, or activity whatever is comparable, rehashing, between or that is common is the common point. Anything familiar after some time or crosswise over the area is common to point. Anything familiar among in close to home endeavors or in aggregate activities is a common point. Along these lines in any event in varying backgrounds or in any move the thing which assumes the focal job is the common point in that activity.

For better understanding, we can say that whatever makes a connection among things by connecting them, builds up contact between them, as a result of which some activity appears is the common point.

For example, in any business element, the personality of the leader of the organization is the common point. The leader through the appeal of his character, and capacities and capabilities tie the team together as well as rouses the team to work more enthusiastically as a result of which the organization advances and the business win higher benefit. In spite of this, if the personality of the leader is feeble, paying little respect to the best of plans and high expertise of work, the results will be the opposite.

People go after things which they consider having esteem. There is a common point or understanding that something is of worth consumption. In spite of this, people coordinate when looked with a mutual threat. This mutual threat is a common point.

Like there are nerves in the body which connect each part of the body with the brain, they take signals from body to brain and directions from brain to body, and go about as common point among body and brain, there are common points in any framework, organization or setup. Through the knowledge of these points, we can dissect, oversee, or enhance the current structure. The most significant frames in our life are our mind.

In any circle of life, our choices shape our lives. These choices are based on our thinking and our analysis of circumstance. Along these lines, it is our thinking that shapes our life. In this view, the most significant activity in our life is thinking. Thinking for analyzing circumstances, and for enhancing new results. If we can demonstrate the significance of common points, show that they assume the focal job in the thinking, we can likewise explain their importance in each battle of life.

Give us a chance to observe something we as a whole experienced in the most recent couple of minutes.

As you are tuning in to this, your mind is handling this data. Did it happen that while tuning in to this, you knew about some word, expression or sentence, and it reminded you of something else? It occurred. Did it not? Although you were tuning in to this address, a part of this address made you recall something different, maybe insignificant.

It happens a great deal. Each time you tune in, read, observe a specific something, another idea springs up in your mind, and the reason it comes is that your brain picks a part of what you are deliberately observing and shapes a bridge between your conscious perception and something else in mind.

Release us through another example to clarify this. Give us a chance to state, your companion comments about the freshness of natural products when you both are in the market. This idea of 'fresh' causes you to recall that another companion requested that you buy a fresh cake for the party. The 'cake' is sweet, so you remember. What's more, eating 'sweet' can cause issues for your 'diabetes' and for keeping your 'diabetes' within proper limits, you ought to routinely take 'medicine.' You recall that your 'medicine' is going to end, and you should 'buy more medicine.' For 'buying more medicine,' you decide to drive to closest restorative store after buying the natural products in this market.

This voyage of contemplations from the freshness of organic products to choosing to drive to medicinal store was conceivable through a progression of points that framed a bridge.

Each time, you go over an idea, a segment of the idea encourages you to recall another idea. In above examples, they are 'fresh', 'cake', 'sweet', 'diabetes', 'take medicine', and 'buy medicine'. These ideas structure a bridge between current idea and quick next idea. Exclusively they are common points between two back to back ideas and all things considered they are a common point between two remote ideas of 'freshness' and 'driving.'

This is how we move, starting with one idea then onto the next. This is the smoothness of a creative mind. It is, likewise, a potent technique for imaginative thinking.

In this example, we recalled things. However, we can likewise confound things, consolidate them, and similarly make new ones. For example, consider yourself making some tea. You include hot water, a tea sack, and sugar in a cup. From 'hot water' you recall drinking 'lemon' with warm water yesterday, just because which was an incredible encounter. Returning to tea, you decide to include some lemon in this blend of warm water with tea. You end up making another tea for yourself. It is black tea with lemon. The common point 'hot water' helped you connect two ideas of black tea and lemon, which were at first discrete.

Indeed, it is a similar way somebody improved cell phones with a camera by observing the common characteristic that both can be held close by. This handheld component was the common point. Maybe, he found this element by some coincidence or due to the longing to take and send a photo to a friend or family member through telephone. Be that as it may, this common point empowered him to join the two machines.

Had cameras being huge like vehicles or had a common point among camera and versatile stayed unobserved, you could never take selfies. How miserable would that be? So once you take a selfie, always remember common points and their power to advance, and concoct.

Be that as it may, is the utilization of common points just constrained to memory recall, and advancement? No. It stretches out to rationale, essential thinking, and analysis of perception.

Like the smoothness, and memory recall, our concepts are covering and blended. A few ideas which part of broader ideas can are frame a bridge between two more general purposes. At times, they can shape the bridge between restricting views and help us to turn the argument against its defender.

For example, somebody contends that 'Everyone has the freedom to do whatever the person wishes. Accordingly, there must not be any confinements whatsoever'. From this argument, it pursues that one isn't confined from suppressing freedom of others. Therefore, as a result, the odds are that there will be at any rate one person who won't have the freedom to do at any price one thing the individual in question wishes. This negates the case that everyone has the freedom to do whatever the person in question wishes.

As should be obvious, the idea that 'one isn't limited from suppressing freedom of others' pursues from the finish of argument 'there must not be any confinements whatsoever' and connects it with the opposite of reason of case 'Everyone has the freedom to do whatever the person in question wishes.' As a result, it is shared between two different ideas.

This is the reason some scholar once commented: Every postulation has seeds of its reputation. In this way, any argument might be flipped completely around, by identifying something inside the premises of the case and utilizing it to create an end that negates the beginning argument.

The job of common points stretches out past simple refutation. They, in reality, make arguments and empower ends. For example, I state: Tech companies are contracting AI experts nowadays. All AI experts will be experts of formal thinking. Accordingly, tech companies are recruiting experts on legal reasoning. By being common between two ideas of Tech companies enlisting an expert of structured thinking, the terms 'artificial intelligence expert' empowers us to close something about the connection of these two ideas.

In any case, due to their convincing power, the common points can be misleading. Think about another argument: Knowledge is power. Power will remain in general corrupt. Consequently, knowledge corrupts.

Here obviously the term 'power' is a common point. However, it has been utilized in two different implications. The power that corrupts is power over people and energy that originates from knowledge is power over one's shortcomings. Hence, it's anything but a common between the two ideas.

Unwary of this double importance, peruse can be betrayed into accepting knowledge is corrupt. This technique of argumentation is utilized by fan leaders, for the most part, religious.

Along these lines, for unwavering discernment, which we should improve, we should identify and refine our comprehension of common points in any argument. For analyzing any case, we should concentrate on the common aspects in it; we should recognize their quality and nonattendance, their definitions and employment.

Just like there can be a similar concept common between two ideas which empower derivation, sometimes we can identify similarities common between two things to finish up something. This is called analogies. For example, this presentation is getting long, like waterway Nile. This length is the common characteristic between the two - my performance and Nile. Along these lines, because of similarity, it tends to be reasoned that I will talk much more. Be that as it may, an excellent presentation ought to resemble a lady's skirt; long enough to cover the subject and short enough to make interest. Along these lines, we can infer that I will complete it soon. In any case, we will see which deduction right, and which analogy is worked in.

In analogies as well, common points of similarities empower us to finish up, and along these lines, these can be beguiling as well. We must, at that point, be cautious when establishing similarities.

Similarities between two things as well as a pattern that is common over a few things encourage us to classify things or make abstractions. For example, we observe that the creatures that breastfeed conceive an offspring instead of lay eggs. Consequently, we sum up that all creatures that breastfeed imagine a family, although a breastfeeding creature may lay an egg. For example, Duck-charged platypus. In this manner, again, common points or common qualities empower us to sum up, however alert is required.

Similarly, if a pattern is common after some time, it tends to be helpful for forecasting or may show a connection of circumstances and logical results, for example, each time the national bank declares something money related market shows expanded unpredictability. One may suggest that the declarations are a reason for developed instability. In any case, such speculations are suggestive just and scarcely convincing.

This way, our whole thinking, our very establishment of life, because our thinking shapes our experience, primarily works given ideas that structure an extension, ideas that are same, similar, or are repeating. These are common between different approaches. In this way, these are common points. It is these common points that enable us to review, enhance, classify, find, or construe.

In short think about a chain attached to a stone. Each link of chain guarantees that the entire string goes about as one unit and empowers you to pull the stone wanted way. Be that as it may, if even one link in chain breaks, you won't probably pick the rock. Just like these links of the chain, our considerations, activities, relations, systems, or anything relies upon those points that empower the association between at least two points. These links are common points. What's more, just like each link of chain associates with a prompt next link, common points interface with quick next one as it were. An absence of a common point between two points implies that they can't cooperate like a system.

Common points represent our thinking. Be that as it may, we can intentionally analyze them for keeping away from any mistakes, and for positively managing and purposely innovating new results. Just like we usually inhale, however, we can intentionally modify cadence of breathing to accomplish specific mental state. We can deliberately utilize the common points, which as of now usually use, to achieve our objectives.

By intentionally watching the common points, refining them, managing them and innovating them, we can analyze, oversee, and enhance anything and everything. We simplify. We decrease each circumstance to one idea. The idea of common points. That is whatever is the same, similar, repeating, and is in the middle of at least two things, activities, time, or ideas.

As the common points assume the focal job in our thinking, and our thinking shapes our life, it is essential to analyze the common points in each circle of life as well. Along these lines for critical thinking, we must refine our understanding of the common aspects.

Presently the question we have to respond to is just one question: What are common points in our present issue circumstance?

For responding to this one question, we have to concentrate on four concepts. We will experience these four concepts presently, before portraying seven steps expected to execute the system for breaking down, managing, or innovating through common points.

First of all, we observe things that are common crosswise over time or people since they are repeating, either after some time or crosswise over people. For example, you wish to publicize your product. Furthermore, you observe that each time there is a football coordinate, most of the people assemble around the TV, even the individuals who might not observe as a rule. Subsequently, you can utilize this reiteration after some time, which is unsurprising, for elevating your product to most people.

In like manner, you may observe a repeating pattern among youngsters in a region. You discover their craving to learn music. If you know music, you have found a conceivable way, either to connect with them or to sell them a few exercises.

Presently something else is to discover anybody or anything familiar between at least two others. For example, the middle people, wholesalers of product market exist between the makers and purchasers. They associate the two, which is a specific capacity. Be that as it may, they crowd to build the costs which are negative capacity. An administration guideline expanded expense or sponsorship, which impact these mediators will change the two purchasers and makers in a roundabout way because the middle people will adjust their conduct appropriately.

Next, you may now observe things that are the same. For example, you may discover that a similar individual who is your neighbor is likewise individual from an examination association that you wish to join. You can request that he direct you and maybe assist you in turning into a part. This individual is, along these lines, typical among you and the association you wish to join.

Like same, another concept is similar. Similarities take into consideration analogies which are incredible methods for either conveying ideas or feeling to the individuals who have not experienced them, or for understanding parts of a thing similar to another.

An example of analogies is verse. Faiz, an artist from Asia, is known for his utilization of analogies. He composed a sonnet for his darling, communicating how he missed her. He stated, in the desert of my isolation, my affection, shudder the shadows of your voice, the mirage of your lips. By utilizing the analogies of a desert, shivering, and mirage he communicated how he missed his cherished such that now any individual who understands the stock point of a desert, quiver, and mirage can get a handle on the force of his longing to join with his adored.

Analogies help us express our ideas to the individuals who have not learned them by utilizing ideas that are commonly understood by us all and have similarities with our thoughts which we wish to express. Along these lines, in correspondence using analogies, there are two common points. One is that all commonly understand ideas used as analogies, and two these ideas utilized as analogies and the concept which we wish to impart utilizing these analogies have common characteristics or everyday points.

Presently the question you must ask is: How would we be able to utilize this idea of common points for breaking down, managing and innovating?

To analyze, oversee, and develop utilizing the common points, we must identify, refine, modify, and expel them. To do as such, we must pose a progression of inquiries. These questions should enable us to identify and improve them before we can modify, expel, or include new points. The objective is to consider whole to be as a lot of common points weave together alongside different positions, and through the understanding of nature of these points, we ought to have the option to see the guide everything being equal, potential outcomes of progress. There is a seven-step process to pursue:

Step 1: Identity:

1st question to ask: What are the common points?

That which is the same, similar, between or repeating in periods, things, spaces, people, ideas and activities, and so forth.

Step 2: Challenge:

- o 1st question to ask: Do we see a common point which in reality does not exist?
- o Challenge your perception by asking: Is that so? Consider the possibility that it isn't.
- o The 2nd question to ask: Are there some common points which we are uninformed of?
- o Step 3: Refine:
- o 1st Question to ask: Is there any equivocalness or unclearness in the understanding of the common points?
- o Recall the example of knowledge is power. The word 'power' was questionable. Every common point must have a clear definition. There must not be any overlapping, fluffy, vague implications.

- The 2nd Question to ask: Do we come up short on some information about common points?
- It is conceivable that some common points are concealed profound inside public perceptions. You need to burrow profound inside.
-
- 3rd Question to ask: Do we confuse at least two common points to be one or overlapping?
- For example, etiquettes of the gathering are a common point between individuals of a culture. Protocols for gathering dear companions are not the same as those for strangers. One may confuse the two etiquettes accepting that after every both stranger and companions are people.
- the fourth Question to ask: Are the common points discovered quickly to the points between which they are familiar?
- For example, let us watch a, b, c, d, and e, and the c is actually in the center of an, and e yet not the common among an, and e. For this situation, b, c, and d are aggregately common between and an,

and e, while b is common among an, and c just like c, is common among band d and d among c and e.

- The point ought to be to knit the entire picture with no missing snippet of information, with no jump and to move from one location to just quick next one with the goal that we can see every one of the conceivable outcomes.

- Recall, the previous example of going to the market of fresh fruits and choosing to drive to purchase the drug. A jump from fresh fruits to driving would not justify why and how we all of a sudden, decided to go to medicine when we are essentially purchasing fresh fruits.

-

- **Step 4: Explain:**

- 1st Question to solicit: What is the idea of the common points?

- Their definitions, capacities, restrictions, and reasons for existence.

-

- **Step 5: Knit the picture:**

- 1st Question to ask: What are the different points between which they are familiar?
- The 2nd Question to ask: How would they identify with different points between which they are familiar?
-
- **Step 6: Innovate and manage:**
- 1st Question to solicit: How can every one of them be altered?
- For example, a simple divider exists between my office room and my library. I wish to have snappy access to the next room. I can alter the divider and make an entryway.
-
- The 2nd Question to ask: How can there be a purposeful presentation of another common point?
- For example, there is no intercom between my room and another room where my dad works. I can include an intercom which will be a common point for speedy correspondence.

- A 3rd Question to ask: How can some common point be kept away from? Or then again, can some of them be erased from the system?
- For example, one of the windows of my room opens towards a school. During the early afternoon break, the children come to the playground and play. This makes much noise. What's more, the window goes about as a common point for enabling this to go to my room. The glass panes of the window were not sound proof. What I did was to purchase new glass panes, which were soundproof and close my windows during the late morning break. Along these lines, I evade the common point which takes into consideration the noise to come in my room when I need to.
-
- **Step 7: The comprehensive view:**
- 1st Question to solicit: What is the picture of the whole circumstance with our knowledge of common points?

o With this first setup, you can distinguish, break down, manage, and innovate any circumstance, or take care of the issue. You have figured out how the common points can be utilized to make and examine contentions, and how these points can be utilized to innovate and manage anything in life. This basic setup outfits you with all that you need for rearranging your life. In any case, valuable knowledge isn't adequate for handy undertakings of life. The utilization of this to specific everyday issues is needed.

o Just like the psyche is the most significant system in our lives, and it is a common point in each activity of our lives, economic activity influences our lives as well. Everyone engages in a commercial activity, be it not revenue driven organization, labor supply, claim the business, or investing. The economic activity influences the rest of the events of our lives. Along these lines, economic activity is another common point in our lives. Since it is central, it is between different activities. It repeatedly influences our life. In economic activity, the primary job is of competition. Regardless of whether it is NGO, or any businessmen contend each other for there is an agreement. The agreement that the money is significant for living, the money is central for our advanced lives as we never again live in crude public clans. In this way, competition is a common point since it is fundamental in economic activity, it is between all businesses in the market, it repeatedly influences all choices, and is same in all types of events. This implies one of the significant common points in life is competition.

o Everyone faces competition in life. In life, it is possible that we fight, or we run until the end of time. If we run, we end up exhausted and unfulfilled. Accordingly, our only alternative is to fight, to struggle, and to contend. In any case, if we are not furnished with apparatuses and knowledge of competition, we free our valuable time and rare assets. We lose competitions as well. Hence, there is a need to learn competition.

CHAPTER FIVE

Critical thinking is a push to create reliable, objective evaluations about what is reasonable for us to accept and disbelieve. Critical thinking makes use of the tools of logic and science because it values skepticism over guilelessness or dogmatism, reason overconfidence, the science of pseudoscience, and rationality over wishful thinking. Critical thinking does not ensure that we will touch base at the truth, yet it does make it significantly more likely than any of the alternatives do.

Clarifying the concept of critical thinking may be more comfortable if we experience some of the key characteristics which are necessary for thinking critically about something:

Open-Mindedness

A person who wishes to ponder something like politics or religion must be open-disapproved. This requires being open to the possibility that in addition to the fact that others are right that you are incorrect. Time after time, people dispatch into a furor of arguments clearly without setting aside any effort to consider they might be mistaken on the matter.

Of course, it is also possible to be too "open-disapproved" because few out of every odd idea is similarly legitimate or has an equivalent shot of being valid. Although we should take into account the possibility that someone is right, we must still necessitate that they offer support for their claims — if they can't or don't, we might be justified in dismissing those claims and going about as if they weren't valid.

Differentiate Emotion and Reason

Regardless of whether we have clear logical and observational reasons for tolerating an idea, we also most likely have emotional and psychological reasons for tolerating it — purposes which we may not be wholly mindful of. It is essential to critical thinking, be that as it may, that we figure out how to separate the two because the latter can easily meddle with the previous.

Our emotional reasons for thinking something may be very understandable, yet if the logic behind the belief is wrong, at that point eventually, we should not consider our belief objective. If we are going to approach our ideas in a skeptical, reasonable way, at that point, we must be happy to set aside our emotions and assess the logic and reasoning on their terms — possibly notwithstanding dismissing our beliefs if they neglect to satisfy logical criteria (see Open-Mindedness).

Content from Knowledge, not Ignorance

Because we frequently have an emotional or other psychological investment in our beliefs, it isn't unusual for people to step forward and attempt to shield those beliefs regardless of whether the logic or evidence for them is feeble. For sure, sometimes people will guard an idea although they don't have a clue about a lot about it — they figure they do, yet they don't.

A person who tries to practice critical thinking, be that as it may, also seeks to abstain from assuming that they know all that they have to know. Such a person will permit that someone who disagrees can show them something significant and refrains from contending a position if they are oblivious of significant, applicable facts.

The likelihood is not Certainty

Some ideas are most likely evident and ideas that are undoubtedly valid, yet while it is pleasant to have an idea that belongs in the latter group, we must understand that the last group is far, far smaller than the previous. Anyway, best it may be. Otherwise, we can't be sure about a considerable amount of matters — especially those matters that are the focus of numerous debates.

At the point when a person exercises skepticism and critical thinking, they recollect that just because they can show a conclusion is most likely evident, that doesn't mean they have taught or can confirm that it is valid. Certain truths require a firm conviction, yet plausible realities require just conditional confidence — in other words, we should trust them with the same strength as the evidence and reason permit.

Stay away from Linguistic Misunderstandings.

Language is a mind-boggling and subtle apparatus. It allows us to impart a wide range of ideas, including spic and span ideas, yet the same subtlety and unpredictability lead to a wide range of misunderstandings, ambiguities, and vagueness. The truth is, the thing that we think we are imparting probably won't be what others are getting, and what we are accepting may not be what others are proposing to convey.

Critical thinking, at that point, must take into consideration the existence of ambiguities, vagueness, and misunderstandings in our communications. A person who tries to think critically must undertake to dispense with those factors as much as possible — for instance, by attempting to get critical terms characterized right off the bat instead of enabling a debate to continue with people using the same words to discuss different concepts.

Maintain a strategic distance from Common Fallacies

Most people can reason all around ok to get by in their everyday lives and no more. If that is sufficient to survive, why invest the additional time and work to improve? People who wish to have elevated expectations for their beliefs and reasoning, be that as it may, can't manage with the absolute minimum to get by in life — more education and practice are required.

To this end, excellent critical thinking requires that a person becomes acquainted with regular logical fallacies which most people submit at some time or other while never acknowledging it. Mistakes are errors in reasoning which creep into arguments and debates steadily; the practice of critical thinking should enable a person to abstain from submitting them and help in identifying their appearance in others' cases. An argument that commits a deception can't give a valid justification to acknowledge its conclusion; in this manner, as long as fallacies are being dedicated, the cases aren't as a rule extremely profitable.

Try not to Jump to Conclusions.

It's natural and normal for people to rapidly go to the first and most obvious conclusion in any situation, yet the truth is the obvious conclusion isn't always the right one. Sadly, when a person adopts a conclusion it very well may be challenging to get them to surrender it for something else — all things considered, nobody wants not to be right, do they

Because it is smarter to keep away from inconvenience than to attempt to escape difficulty once in it, critical thinking emphasizes cautious thinking as well — and this means not making a hasty judgment if you can stay away from it. Feel free to recognize the existence of an obvious conclusion because it may be right all things considered; however, don't embrace it until other options have been found.

The majority of this is just a speedy summary of some key attributes which people must develop to ponder things. Although it may not seem promptly obvious, you needn't bother with a degree in philosophy or science to improve as a critical mastermind. Some education about fundamental issues is required, however nothing that the average person can't deal with.

Some facets of basic logic may appear to be complicated; however, at last, there is just a single method to end up OK with it: practice. You won't, for instance, become great at perceiving fallacies only by remembering a list of names. Instead, you have to set aside the effort to peruse arguments cautiously and figure out how to identify errors that way. The additional time you spend on that, the more usual, it will move toward becoming — and you will recall the names of the fallacies as a matter of course.

The same is valid for other concepts in basic logic. If you consider them and use them, at that point, you'll feel good with them and perceive specific argumentative strategies and techniques in anything you read without genuinely attempting. The precise wording will track with without anyone else. If you are interested in the practice, one great spot to discover help is this site's forum. There you will get an opportunity to peruse lots of arguments and see a considerable lot of the techniques described on this site set in motion. You can also ask questions about the legitimacy or soundness of specific cases — there are a lot of people who can assist you with understanding better where an argument goes wrong or gets things right.

Most people think being smart is tied in with having more facts. Trivia-shows like Jeopardy! Epitomize this view of knowledge. The most intelligent people are the people with the most names, dates, and places stored away inside their mind.

This is probably the least essential and useful part of learning, however. Instead of facts, I'd prefer to focus on knowledge that acts as tools. The more you have, the more ways you can approach different problems.

This is a topic that has been discussed a lot before. However, I'd like to take a different edge at it.

Professions as Thinking Toolkits

Most people define professions by what those professions do. Engineers build things. Economists study money. Psychologists investigate people's minds.

However, while this is a noticeable distinction, I'm more interested not in what types of problems professions try to solve, yet how they try to solve them. Here, we can uncover an abundance of different thinking tools that are frequently abstract enough to apply well outside the common interest of the profession.

Consider economics. Albeit most people view this as a study of money, it is more like a way of thinking about the world. Henceforth we have books like Freakonomics which apply the thinking tools of economics to a wide range of scenarios that have nothing to do with money.

thirty-three Thinking Tools

The following are twenty-five tools. I've abstracted from the profession I feel exemplifies the best.

1. Artist: What if Creativity Were the Priority?

Artist

Most other professions are loaded with constraints upon one's ideas. They need to be monetizable, mathematical, under budget, and within specifications. Artists operate in a realm where most of these constraints are reduced, so the bigger question is, "For what reason is this unique and interesting?"

This, however, is a useful thinking tool to apply to numerous other concerns. Frequently the best companies produce things that resemble art. They are driven by uniqueness and creativity, rather than blandly filling out a list of specs.

How would your work change if you made curiosity the most significant priority? How could your goals and projects be different if coolness, interestingness, or refinement of an original idea were your priority?

2. Economist: How Do People React to Incentives?

There are many thinking tools native to economics, yet a foundational one is simple. People respond to incentives.

Tyler Cowen, the economist, delivers this best, explaining a key component of economic reasoning is that by changing a system involving people, the people do not stay in place. Instead, they respond to the new incentives accordingly.

Almost any action you'll take alters the perceptions of incentives by other people you deal with. The economist in you should ask yourself, "if I change this, by what means will people react?"

3. Engineer: Can I Model This and Calculate?

Engineering, being built off the hard sciences, has some of the most precise and accurate estimates in any profession. While your financial advisor can throw darts at picking which stocks will rise, and a psychologist can give hints at what people will do, engineers routinely create things which don't currently exist and need to work 100% of the time.

The essence of doing this is to create a model of what you're trying to work with, measure the relevant variables, and know to what degree of error you can expect in those measurements. From there, you can realize what will occur, instead of just guessing.

My group and I applied this recently to a problem we had involving predicting our sales. We decided to make a model of sales numbers based on to what extent people had subscribed and how regularly they had been offered an opportunity to sign up. From there, we will almost certainly make much better estimates of our sales, whereas our guesses before would regularly be wildly off the mark.

4. Entrepreneur: Do a Lot of Things; See What Works

Entrepreneurs frequently have too little money, resources, support, or time. However, they need to scramble together a solution that will somehow make money. They can do this by adopting a set of thinking tools that is regularly rare for regular professionals.

One primary tool is rapid prototyping. Numerous people see this as a product development strategy. You make something that barely works to see if anybody wants it. In any case, in reality, it's an abstract thinking tool that applies to a lot more than product R&D.

The essence of this thinking tool is that you go out and try a lot of things, without waiting around for a perfect answer. It also requires listening carefully for feedback, so you can get hints as to what to do straight away. Speed and volume make okay with making decisions in a noisy environment loaded with uncertainty.

Sometimes the right way to solve a problem is to do a lot of things and see what works!

5. Doctor: What's the Diagnosis?

Doctors meet patients who have an array of symptoms, some of which they probably aren't telling you (or can't). From there, you need to act like a detective to deduce the most likely disease and create an arrangement to cure it. During this, a wrong move might kill your patient, so you need to choose wisely.

A useful thinking tool from medicine is the idea of using symptoms to deduce a disease and comparing with base rates to make highly accurate decisions.

While this applies to medicine, there's a lot of places where the diagnosis is essential. Your car is making a funny noise. Your computer doesn't work. Your business has stopped making money.

The first thing to do is to see what all the possible causes could be. This requires study and knowledge. Next, you need to rule out as numerous as possible based on the symptoms you observe. Finally, of the options that are left, which are rare afflictions, and which are relatively normal? Knowing this can enable you to settle on a most likely diagnosis.

6. Journalist: Just the Facts

Journalists rely on a vast amount of different thinking tools which enable them to write compelling stories that report the news fairly and accurately.

One of these thinking tools is actuality checking. Because journalists frequently need to interview sources who might mislead (or even hostile), it's essential to corroborate information exchanged from independent sources. Reality checking might be time-consuming; however, it results in a considerably more accurate worldview than merely blindly following a stray remark.

How would your life look if you dug around to check the integrity of critical pieces of information you depend on to make decisions? Imagine if you had to report what you know in the New York Times. Would it need to be retracted later?

7. Scientist: Make a Hypothesis and Test It

Scientists discover truths about the world. To do this, they need thinking tools.

An essential thinking tool of science is the controlled experiment. Keep every one of the variables the same, except the one you want to test, and see what happens. This requires meticulous preparation and design to prevent outside contamination from breaking your results.

Too numerous people draw inferences from "experiments" that are anything but. They have many conflicting variables that make making determinations about their experiences significantly more difficult. What if you moved toward your diets like a scientist? You're working routines? Okay still trust them after.

What number of your beliefs about work and life withstand such scrutiny? Experience such testing? Possibly you could benefit from a little increasingly scientific thinking tools in your life.

8. Mathematician: You Don't Know Until You Can Prove It

The thinking tools of a mathematician rely upon having a lot higher standard of what constitutes a proof of something. While a specialist may tolerate precision within some bounds, and an entrepreneur might be satisfied with a hunch, a mathematician's statements must be irrefutable, or they don't count.

One way you can see this thinking tool impact non-mathematical domains is in an adjacent field such as programming. During my MIT Challenge, I heard lecturers talk about the MIT style of programming versus the one originating out of Bell Labs. MIT, which was increasingly mathematical and scholarly, tended to be progressively rigorous in demonstrating its programs worked, while Bell Labs was often content with an algorithm which seemed to carry out the responsibility, regardless of whether they couldn't guarantee it.

Mathematical thinking tools help you be progressively rigorous and spot mistakes, which may turn out to be relevant.

9. Programmer: What's the Pattern I Can Automate?

Programming encompasses a lot of thinking tools, but the most basic one is the algorithm. Algorithms are a set of steps that can be characterized precisely so that they require no intelligence to play out everyone, yet the net result is a useful product.

A useful application of this is to take a gander at the things you do and see which could be automated, simplified, or refactored. Programmers can spot repeated code and try to abstract out the essence of what is redundant into something that can do what you need automatically.

Past just having the option to write the code yourself, you can think increasingly like a programmer in numerous other domains of life. What things do you often repeat in your work which could be automated? What ambiguous process might you be able to convert into a secure set of steps?

10. Architect: Envisioning the Future

Architects need to design buildings. These are enormous structures which may take years to assemble, and nonetheless meet every one of the criteria of clients, contractors, city planners, and construction laws. Gracious, and they should also be beautiful.

To do this, architects need a suite of thinking tools (and software) to take a thought and envision what it will resemble, correctly, on an enormous scale, after millions of dollars have been spent. One of those tools is merely making a model.

Making a scaled-down version of the thing you want to create, so you can see what it looks like, and after that envisioning how it will be on a bigger version is difficult, but it often lets you see how reality will be before it's too late to transform it.

11. Salesperson: Understand Their Minds Better than They Do

Selling often gets negative criticism. People think it's about trickery and deceit as you try to be manipulating someone into purchasing something they likely shouldn't.

Although this is the stereotype, the actual reality is once in a while like this. Instead, salespeople work to profoundly understand what the customer needs, and after that match them with products and services that fill that void. This is unbelievably difficult to do, as you may perceive that you have the solution to a customer's problem before they do.

A vital thinking tool for success in this profession is to have the option to infer what people's worries and needs are by their (often contradictory conduct). What language do they use? How do their actions differ from their stated intentions? What would you be able to infer about this?

This is a tool you can apply a long way past making an extra commission. What does your spouse truly want, rather than what they're telling you? What about your friends? Your boss?

12. Soldier: Routine and Discipline Prevent Deadly Mistakes

The discipline exemplified by military personnel is a useful thinking tool, even outside of combat situations. Training and routine become a safeguard against careless mistakes which could cost lives. By requesting an adjustment to those protocols, notwithstanding when there is no peril, there is significantly less space for slip-ups.

Making your bed each morning may not forestall casualties, yet if you can follow that methodology consummately, you'll also be bound to follow the ones that may save your life. This sort of discipline is also present in another live-endangering field: prescription.

The Checklist Manifesto takes this idea of military routine and applies it to unremarkable things like handwashing, which save lives by keeping away from disease.

When you realize the best method to accomplish something, do it precisely and precisely, without sloppiness or somebody may get injured.

13. Chess Master: See the Moves in Your Mind's Eye

Chess has, for some time, been considered a game to improve one's thinking. While it's suspicious that years of chess study will necessarily make you smarter, there are a lot of thinking tools which can be mined from the game.

One is the ability to simulate the game in your mind's eye. A typical trap of grandmasters is making blindfolded games. While this amazes spectators, it reinforces a useful practice—being ready to see the game in your mind, so you can ascertain future moves your rival makes.

This is frequently useful in different domains outside of chess. Attempting to visualize what may occur, and afterward contrast that expectation with the real world. This can sharpen your simulation abilities, so when you're in a difficult situation, you'll have the option to anticipate what happens straightaway.

14. Designer: The Things You Make Communicate For You

One of my preferred books is The Design of Everyday Things. While this book is intended for designers, it is hugely a book of thinking tools designers should develop. As such, it's something you can get and peruse regardless of whether you've never made anything in your life.

A useful tool here is how something is made on how to use it. A well-designed entryway handle suggests push or draw, without needing to say it. A well-designed light switch should as of now disclose to you which rooms will be lit up when you flip it.

Imagine a scenario where you designed your speeches so that they consequently caused the group of spectators to shift their thinking where you need them to go. Imagine a situation where you created your habits so that you, therefore, connected them. The scope of this thinking tool is extensive.

15. Teacher: Can You See What it is Like Not to Know Something Obvious?

How would you make knowledge inside someone else's mind? How might you give them abilities they didn't have previously?

Most of us underestimate how stunning instructing is, and our very own ability to learn from it. To be viable, teachers need to have a model of how their pupil's minds see the world, as well as a game arrangement for evolving it.

To succeed in most professions, you need to have the option to make other people see the problems as you do. This involves identifying what knowledge they need and saying the right things to get them where you are present. While this is a distinct skill for teachers, it also benefits programmers attempting to clarify their code, doctors trying to explain the reasons for a therapeutic method or a pioneer who wants employees to follow a vision.

16. Anthropologist: Can You Immerse and Join Another Culture?

Anthropology is the study of cultures. In contrast to economics, which tends to focus on numerical models, or psychology, which tends to complete a lot of cautious experiments, anthropologists learn about cultures by really immersing in them.

How might you immerse yourself in groups to which you don't have a place? Groups of different nationalities or languages? Politics or professions? Hobbies, sports, religions, or philosophies? How might you learn how those groups of people function, have them acknowledge you as you live alongside them?

17. Psychologist: Test Your Understanding of Other People

Psychology has different thinking tools inserted both in its assumptions about human instinct, as well as in its methods for discovering it.

On the subject of psychology itself, there are countless tools. Psychological biases, models of consideration, decent quality, preferences, instincts, memory, and that's only the tip of the iceberg. Dozens of books could be composed on the most proficient method to contemplate other people by using these tools, and there have been.

Interestingly, psychology is also a profession with its own set of tools for discovering psychology. Like all scientists, this involves doing experiments where you can control everything except the variable you need to study. In contrast to different scientists, be that as it may, your object of study are individuals, which means you regularly can't tell them what you're attempting to adjust.

18. Critic: Can You Build on The Work of Others?

Numerous critics go past disclosing to your which books to peruse and which movies to watch. They assemble analysis, elucidation, and discussion that go well past the first work.

The thinking tools included are very significant, notwithstanding for people who don't examine writing professionally. For starters, there is the ability to give very close consideration to imaginative works. I am encountering something substantially more profoundly than just a shallow consumer. Second, there's the tool of being ready to interface that knowledge to a trap of different issues and ideas. This builds on a unique creation to include more insight and ideas that were there initially.

19. *Philosopher: What are the Unexpected Consequences of an Intuition?*

Philosophers, at least the analytical kind, tend to have a similar style and toolkit as mathematicians, except often in dealing with things that are based in imprecise words. As a result, there's a lot of useful thinking tools for dealing with matters that can't be decreased to numbers.

One useful asset has the option to see the unexpected consequences of stretching an idea to its limits. This has two benefits. First, it can uncover flaws in the first idea, by reduction ad absurdum. Second, this can enable you to perceive the fundamental principles behind your unclear intuitions of things. By exposing your plans to stronger, hypothetical critiques, you can see what the exact mechanisms by which they work.

20. Accountant: Watch the Ratios

Money is the blood of a business. Accounting is the work that watches how it flows around, checking to make sure it isn't getting obstructed.

There are several useful thinking tools from accounting that permit the diagnosis of problems which are covered up on the surface. One of these is the idea of ratio analysis. Ratios are a fraction with a numerator and denominator of two different measurements inside a business. The leverage ratio, for instance, is the debt the organization owes to the equity put in by the owners. Get too high, and there's a greater risk of default. Value earnings ratio tells you how expensive stock is based on its profits.

This kind of analysis (and numerous others from accounting) is useful to non-accounting domains. In healthy, BMI is a kind of extravagant ratio analysis. In this case, it's your weight contrasted with your height squared. But you could also envision tracking many other numbers and their ratios: output every hour worked, bugs per lines of code, date every hour spent on internet dating.

Arranging the data, monitoring the details, and seeing the patterns beneath the surface are on the whole accounting tools you can exploit outside of a spreadsheet.

21. Politician: What Will People Believe?

Politics offers its own set of tools. A noteworthy difference between politics and business is that while both are gone for accomplishing some objective in the world—the previous depends exceedingly on the impression of voters. A business can work, whereas a politician may work admirably, and still get kicked out because of bad PR.

Therefore, the thinking tools possessed by politicians are about calculating not just the effect of some action, but also on how that action will be seen — both by the voting masses, and one's allies and enemies.

The thinking tools here imply that sometimes the right decision isn't possible, simply because other people won't see it as such, and you can't persuade them. This might frustrate, but it applies to numerous parts of reality we'd instead it didn't.

22. Novelist: Does Your Story Make Sense?

Numerous people see stories as the linguistic embodiment of history. We take what occurred and mesh it into some words so others can see it for themselves.

Novelists understand better than anybody that what happens is often not a decent story. Stories have characters with fixed traits that make their actions predictable. People are more affected by context.

Stories have beginnings, middles, and ends. Reality is a continuous stream of events without a bend.

Unfortunately, people understand stories much better than realities. So often you have to bundle up the histories you want to tell people such that they can interpret. Who is included? When did those things occur? Offer information to make it easier for the listener to pursue.

While this applies to write novels or to make movies, to tell stories is a part of everyone's life. From "For what reason would you like to work at this specific employment," to, "Where do you see yourself in five years?" These are on the whole stories, and we have to understand their structures.

23. Actor: The Best Way to Pretend is to Be Real

A well-known thinking tool for acting is called strategy acting. This system includes attempting to feel the feelings of the character you're depicting, instead of merely faking it.

This may appear to be a logical inconsistency: how might you feel something you know is fake? Be that as it may, this gives a false representation of how amazing the creative mind is to conjure up circumstances to create compassion. Past battles can remain set up for the actions of the job you play. Dread, bliss, confidence, and enthusiasm all look better when you're encountering it.

Which likewise proposes a ground-breaking thinking tool, although this one is fuller of feeling than psychological: changing your enthusiastic state to get the results you need. Feeling insecure, yet realize you lack confidence? For what reason wouldn't you be able to call that up in yourself as though you have an influence? Be that as it may, don't fake it–feel it.

24. Plumber: Take it Apart and See What's Broken

Tradespeople don't get enough credit for having one of a kind problems fathoming tools and systems. Many Many academic and scholarly sorts could never think about a career in plumbing, carpentry or electrical work. However, those professions regularly out-procure those with advanced education, and in light of current circumstances: they are hard skills which are sought after.

The pith of plumbing, much the same as numerous different exchanges, is to get your hands dirty and dismantle something to perceive what's broken. To do this, you need a model of what's in there else you may get water spilling everywhere or a perilous stun. Be that as it may, you additionally need to dismantle things to understand them.

What number of us abstain from understanding things because we're hesitant to get our hands dirty? We don't have any desire to hazard breaking something, so we never really know how it works?

25. Hacker: What's Going on Underneath?

Hacking is a standout amongst the most generally misconstrued skills. TV programs depict it as a sort of computer enchantment, with flying 3D squares and firewall health bars which go down to zero.

In practice, in any case, hacking is for the most part about understanding that there is regularly a more convoluted layer of directions which a more straightforward layer is based on top. A computer sits in pecking orders, so each level of deliberation simplifies and reduces the thickness beneath to make it clearer. Be that as it may, in some cases this can enable you to do things which look impossible to a higher level, however, are an unintended feature of how the lower level works.

One case of this is a memory flood abuse. Numerous projects work on a higher level whereby memory is gotten to in restricted storehouses. Request something outside of, and you'll get a blunder. Be that as it may, in practice, the mind all sits on a significant line, with memory for different things alongside one another. If you can compose memory "outside of the limits" you can get the computer to do things you'd naively expect were impossible.

Consider this glitch in a Mario game whereby a progression of sources of info composes the code to an unintended area of the game, enabling you to win by contributing an abnormal succession of activities:

This thinking tool works for computers, yet besides, different areas of life. Remember: everything you see is typically a simplification of a more profound reality. Which can imply that the fundamental framework might be broken in a manner you wouldn't naively expect.

Last Thoughts on Thinking Tools

These are only synopses of a critical tool from different professions. In reality, notwithstanding, there are handfuls, if not hundreds of thinking tools for every space of skill. Professions, yet side interests, subjects, and general life skills likewise create thinking tools.

The problem is that individuals frequently have a difficult time recognizing the skill and abstracting it far from where it was produced. This is a problem of far exchange, and it is difficult to resolve.

Be that as it may if you can state what the example is, you can begin to perceive how you could apply it elsewhere. The majority of these tools won't work best in areas far outside their beginning zones. A novelist attempting to use narrating to analyze therapeutic problems will be stuck in an unfortunate situation. Frequently we stall out utilizing the preferred tools that we don't significantly think about which ones could apply. Creative solutions require unique thinking, making us consider one tool when we need others.

Creative Work Requires Diverse Thinking Tools

A great trial demonstrates the need for tools like these. Subjects were solicited to use a box from tacks to attach a candle to the divider. The solution was to use the table as a base—attempting to apply to connect directly to the candle just made a wreck. This is hard because we think about the box as a compartment for the tools, not a tool all by itself.

Likewise, vast numbers of these tools may take into account creative solutions to problems you probably won't have considered. For example:

- If you're an entrepreneur, what might your business resemble if you moved toward it like a craftsman, or an instructor, or a novelist?
- If you're a software engineer, how might your code improve if you took the tools of a sales rep or bookkeeper?
- If you're a writer, what might change about your pieces if acted like a researcher, market analyst, or plumber?

Only one out of every odd blend will be useful. However, many may very well give you the solution that will prompt a breakthrough.

Creative Problem Solving

In this way, you have a problem that you need to solve snappily. You have obsessed about this issue for quite a long time, days, months, or even years despite everything you can't resolve it. Don't stress my companion; the answer is as of now inside you. You need to call forward your creative energy to bring the answer into your engaged mind.

How would you do this? It is simple. You use creative problem solving, that is the secret. Creative what?

Creative problem-solving. Creative problem solving is the incredible demonstration of using inside out-of-the-box creativity to solve everyday problems.

Anybody may do the creativity that is as of now within you, and fortunately, it very well with a problem. It matters not if you're a little child or a cheeky attractive resident, it matters not if you are a housewife or a neurosurgeon, you can solve problems creatively, and you can do it without worrying. You should pursue this fundamental creative problem-solving step:

1. Picture ultimate achievement. Don't harp on negative speculation for doing as such will block your creative energy. Instead, you ought to always delight in the way that the answer is as of now inside you. You need to pull it forward from your creative mind. Envisioning disappointment will block your creative energy, and picturing achievement will bring it forward.

2. Be still and realize that the answer is inside you. There is no need to expect that the problem can't be solved. The answer will arrive at you if you quit

stressing and adopt a progressively loosened up strategy. Be tranquil and still and enable the creative plans to approach. What's more, always be eager to sit still and let your thoughts wonder openly.

3. Be persistent. Don't surge the creative problem-solving process. It sometimes takes some time for your creativity to solve a problem, so don't wind up baffled if the issue isn't resolved immediately. Instead, enjoy the creative process for what it truly is, an internal process and be open and responsive to enabling those new answers for approach.

4. Create a positive environment. The creative mind thrives in stable and positive air, so if you are experiencing considerable difficulties creatively solving a problem, then you may need to create an increasingly positive and uplifting environment. This should be possible by tidying up, including plants, consuming aromatherapy candles, or doing whatever you can to create a creative and positive environment. For the first time, you have a creative environment set up; your creative problem-solving abilities will blast forward.

5. Remove time. If conceivable, remove some time to permit your creative problem-solving capacities indeed to emerge. Sometimes you need a difference in landscape and other times you need time away. Be that as it may, you should be happy to give your soul what it needs, a mini vacation to deal with your thoughts and think of the ideal arrangement.

6. Engage others in the creative process. If you stall out and can't escape a groove, it might be a smart thought to talk about your problem with others. Sometimes they can give creativity problem-solving procedures that will support you. They may likewise have the option to solve the problem for you. The significant thing anyway is to enroll the assistance of similar and positive individuals like you. You don't have any desire to request that somebody help that will ingrain negative energy into your mind.

7. Contemplate. Meditation is a standout amongst the ideal ways to engage your creative problem-solving abilities. By hoisting yourself to a different dimension of awareness, you become progressively articulated with

your manners of thinking and can genuinely observe the association superior to anything when you are diverted. Consequently, meditation is an extraordinary way to engage in creative problem-solving.

By following the above essential advances, you can and will creatively solve any problem that may come your way. You'll solve problems with certainty and less worry than if you pursued customary strategies. Along these lines, enjoy the problem-solving process by utilizing creative problem-solving procedures now and for the remainder of your life!

Problem Solving and Decision Making

Problem-solving and decision making is a standout amongst the essential skills required by managers. It is an exceedingly significant skill for managers and leaders since they are the ones who make the decisions in the working environment. Problem-solving and decision making are additionally considered to be one of the hardest skills to ace in the business.

·Define and Analyze the Problem: Problems, clashes, and misjudging happen in the work environment day by day. Before we can decide on the best way to take care of the problem, we should initially know and characterize, and identify the problem itself. When the problem has been detected, we ought to likewise take a gander at the wellsprings of the said problems, who are the general population included?

·Look for a solution: A typical error in solving a problem is that managers and leaders attempt to take care of the problem right away without genuinely thinking about it and without considering every one of the potential outcomes and options. Issues ought not to be illuminated promptly with no musings, particularly the extremely perplexing one. There are numerous techniques on solving problems and which incorporates:

Conceptualizing: Collaborate with associates in thinking of solutions to tackle the problem. Consider different courses on how to deal with the issues identified. It is significant that you additionally tune in and hear out what the other team members need to state. Arrange and bargain to take care of the problem rapidly.

SWOT Analysis: SWOT analysis is a standout amongst the most well-known techniques utilized in problem-solving. It includes knowing the different qualities, shortcomings, openings, and mixed methods. It fills in as a blueprint or a rule that managers, leaders, and team members follow to see unmistakably or oversee well the problem.

Pros and Cons: Every solution has its focal points and detriments. Posting the pros and cons of solving the problem can be extremely useful. It can help weigh out different solutions and advantages to every answer and doing this can help tackle the problem all the more effectively.

· Select the best way to deal with taking care of the problem: This is the place decision making comes in. Select the best decision or option for your question. Focus on a resolution and set your game-plan. After everything has been resolved, make beyond any doubt to follow along and screen prospects. Make beyond any doubt that everything is running smoothly and that the problem has indeed been solved.

The problems and clashes you unravel and the decisions that you make can have an enormous effect and can by and large influence the entire development, procedure, and advancement of your organization.

CONCLUSION

Let's envision I present you with the chance to win money. You should pick a red jellybean from a bowl while blindfolded. You have two alternatives, one dish has just 1 red jellybean with 9 white ones, and the other bowl has 10 red jellybeans with 90 white ones. Which container would you pick to have a superior shot?

A great many people chose the bigger bowl with the one hundred jellybeans. You have a similar probability (10%) to pick a red jellybean in either bowl. This example depends on an investigation directed by Kirkpatrick and Epstein (1992). The aftereffect of the research bolsters that our reasoning isn't as balanced in all circumstances. How often have you said to yourself, "I have a hunch about this?" We will, in general, depend on instinct and heretics (easy mental routes dependent on experience) to assess circumstances.

Some portion of creating basic reasoning includes seeing how our predispositions and defective rationale reduce us from accurate information. Examples of nonsensical reasoning incorporate when we imagine that if two objects contact, they will pass the properties to one another (Law of a virus). Voodoo dolls share this idea; it is accepted that babes with hair from someone else will share the person's properties. Another silly reasoning is when people accept that since two objects look like another object, they share some essential properties (Law of closeness).

When we assess information, we have to do it without including inaccurate suppositions. For example, you see a person strolling with specific papers and some coffee and all of a sudden, the person drops the coffee, and it sprinkles all over them. If the person at that point begins reviling and crying, we may think this person is awkward and mean. What we may overlook is that this person may encounter different things that may influence his/her overcompensation, similar to a darling's demise or joblessness. The inclination for individuals to accentuate personality-based clarifications for conduct is known as the Fundamental Attribution Error.

We have to adjust our psyche to comprehend what intellectual traps we may have before assessing information. At the point when our analysis is joined with an investigation for the information, probability analysis, and grounded rationale, we can be increasingly accurate with our translation. The more accurate the analysis, the more we will profit by our choices.

Necessary Thinking is a created methodology. We should practice it every day with the goal for us to turn out to be better at it. I trust this arrangement has helped you and has given you a look at how we can improve ourselves every day.

CPSIA information can be obtained
at www.ICGtesting.com
Printed in the USA
BVHW041937091120
592889BV00013B/185